The Homiletic of All Believers

A Conversational Approach to Proclamation and Preaching

O. Wesley Allen Jr.

WESTMINSTER
JOHN KNOX PRESS
LOUISVILLE · KENTUCKY

Scripture quotations from the New Revised Standard Version of the Bible are copyright © 1989 by the Division of Christian Education of the National Council of the Churches of Christ in the U.S.A. and are used by permission.

Book design by Sharon Adams
Cover design by Lisa Buckley
Cover photograph: Stephanie Dalton Cowan/Getty Images

First edition
Published by Westminster John Knox Press
Louisville, Kentucky

This book is printed on acid-free paper that meets the American National Standards Institute Z39.48 standard. ∞

PRINTED IN THE UNITED STATES OF AMERICA

05 06 07 08 09 10 11 12 13 14—10 9 8 7 6 5 4 3 2 1

Library of Congress Cataloging-in-Publication Data

Allen, O. Wesley.
    The homiletic of all believers : a conversational approach / O. Wesley Allen, Jr.
        p. cm.
    Includes bibliographical references.
    ISBN 0-664-22860-7 (alk. paper)
    1. Preaching. 2. Conversation—Religious aspects—Christianity. I. Title.

    BV4211.3.A425 2005
    251—dc22   2004057242

Contents

Acknowledgments

It has taken me several years to complete this book. I began in the Forest and finished in the Bluegrass, and many people gave me aid on the journey. Colleagues, pastors, students, friends, and family were willing to read drafts of my writing and enter into serious conversation with me about my ideas. I cannot fully express how much better they made this work, but I do wish to thank publicly Todd Allen (who is related to me but wishes he wasn't), Jon Berquist, Jeff Campbell, Russell Compton, Wayne Croft, Virginia Dinsmore, Heather Murray Elkins, Mariah Hayden, Scott Rollins, Jerry Sumney, and Lynne Westfield.

A special word of thanks is also due to several individuals for other contributions to this project and to my well-being during the time I have worked on it. Both Dean Maxine Clarke Beach of Drew Theological School and President R. Robert Cueni of Lexington Theological Seminary not only supported this work but also were extremely supportive of me as a person in a trying time of transition. I hope to be able to repay their acts of kindness some day. Upon his retirement from Drew University, Charles Rice graciously extended my conversation circle in the field of homiletics by giving me a portion of his library. A number of these works have found places in the endnotes of this manuscript. Ron Allen (who is not related to me but wishes he was), of Christian Theological Seminary, has been my most engaged conversation partner throughout this project. He has offered helpful suggestions and even more helpful encouragement. I am especially pleased that he has written the foreword for this book, which relates to a small element of his extensive contributions to the field of homiletics. Tzu Lun Tsai, a graduate student in liturgical studies and homiletics at Drew University, served as my research assistant and conversation partner for the first half of this work. Without her help uncovering the materials dealing with pedagogical theory used in chapter 2, this book may have never taken shape. Stephanie Egnotovich, at Westminster John Knox Press, has offered significant encouragement and critique and has wielded her red pen with great skill to smooth my writing into a much more readable text. My students and clergy attending continuing education events have provided feedback to different portions of my work at different stages of its development. I am especially grateful to have had the opportunity to share some of my thoughts with and hear responses from the entire seminary community at LTS in my inaugural lecture.[1] And, as always, my closest conversation partner has been my wife, Bonnie Cook. She has not only read and responded to various drafts but has been continually supportive of this and all my work.

Finally, I wish to thank my parents, my first conversation partners. My family of origin was a family of talkers. I especially remember with joy some of the heated theological conversations we had when I was a teenager. My faith has changed dramatically over the years, yet those conversations, to a great extent, set the direction for the journey I would travel as a Christian, as a preacher, and as a scholar. Therefore, I dedicate this book to my father, Oscar W. Allen, and to my mother, Marilyn B. Allen.

O. Wesley Allen Jr.
Pentecost 2004

Foreword

In this exciting and pioneering book, O. Wesley Allen invites us to understand preaching as conversation. Moreover, he roots this approach in an ecclesiology of the church as a community of conversation whose purpose is to come to a persuasive interpretation of God's purposes for the world and to mobilize for participation in those purposes. The idea of the sermon as a conversation, then, is not simply a style or form of preaching; it is an integral expression of the nature and purpose of the church.

By "preaching as conversation," Allen does not mean that the time in the service of worship designated for the sermon should be one when members talk out loud with one another. Rather, he intends that the preacher's words in the pulpit have the character of conversation with the congregation. To accomplish this, the minister, though speaking in monologue, constructs the sermon as an exploration of a text, doctrine, or situation with the give-and-take among different voices that marks genuine conversation. Through attentive listening to multiple voices in the Bible, Christian tradition, congregation, and beyond, the preacher seeks to help the congregation come to the most adequate interpretation of the presence and purposes of God that they can at the moment.

Furthermore, in a bold and pioneering proposal, Allen calls for sermons over weeks and months to be in conversation with one another. Preachers sometimes think that when they have mentioned a matter in the pulpit, they have dealt adequately with it. However, Allen reminds us that congregations (like individuals and households) often mull issues, ideas, feelings, and decisions over long periods of time. In this vein, Wes Allen outlines a practical approach to preaching in which sermons are in conversation with one another over a season or more of the church's life.

Allen's nuts-and-bolts plan in chapter 5 is the most comprehensive attempt in the current literature on preaching to help preachers consciously prepare sermons that will have a cumulative effect over time. Along the way, a part of the vocation of the preacher is to name and facilitate conversations taking place in the broader life of the congregation and to bring them into dialogue with one another. As necessary, the preacher engages in critical reflection; injects new voices into the mix; and reinforces, reframes, or blows the whistle on some conversations while starting others.

The notion of preaching as conversation is particularly well suited to our time, for it interacts positively with four qualities that are commonplace in the postmodern ethos of the early twenty-first century. First is a respect for pluralism fueled by the notion that each person and community is an Other whose integrity is to be honored. Second, awareness of the relativity of all claims results from the fact that we know that all perception is conditioned by our own social locations, and that we can never perceive reality in a pure, completely objective, and uninterpreted way. All perception is relative. Third, postmodern communities name and deconstruct the ways that statements, policies, and practices privilege certain groups (often at the expense of others). And finally, many postmoderns are more willing than were many moderns to converse with voices from the past in the hope of encountering wisdom to help us make our way through pluralism and relativity.

A conversational homiletic respects Others (such as biblical texts and other communities) and listens for insights they might have into God's intentions for our time. Conversational preaching aims to help a congregation identify those qualities in God, community, and mission on which a congregation can count while not idolizing those very things. Since we cannot achieve absolute and objective apprehension, especially when discerning God's leading, a conversational approach to preaching helps us identify and say clearly what we can believe and what we think we are supposed to do while recognizing that further conversation may help us reshape our thinking. The postmodern era is ripe for church and culture to give a fresh hearing to the voices in the Bible.

Moreover, while we sometimes think of preaching as conversation as a new idea, its spirit is as old as the Bible itself. Without putting too much weight on this observation, we note that our word "homily" comes from the Greek verb *homileō*, which referred in antiquity to conversation, give and take, about matters of importance.[1] Although the Second Testament never uses *homileō* specifically for preaching, we can see the importance of conversation as a way of helping people interpret the significance of

God's action for the world through Jesus Christ (Luke 24:14–15; Acts 20:11; 24:11).

Much more significant is the fact that the process of writing the books of the Bible often had the quality of conversation. The biblical writers, in their different times and contexts, brought stories, laws, songs, wisdom sayings, and other material from the past into dialogue with their current situations in order to offer interpretations of God's purposes that were consistent with the tradition they had inherited and that also took into account the current circumstances and ways of thinking. For example, at a time when the Deuteronomic theology insisted that obedience begets blessing and disobedience results in curse, the writer of Job told the story of the ancestral figure of the same name who was obedient but who suffered mightily. The experience of Job calls into question the theological equation of the Deuteronomists. In essence, the writer of Job provokes a conversation about how most adequately to understand the relationship of God: obedience, disobedience, blessing, and curse. In a similar way, the writings of Paul are part of a conversation. The apostle was sparked to write by situations and conversations in the congregations; the letters are the records we have of Paul's contributions to those dialogues. Unfortunately we do not have access to an important phase of the conversational life of those letters in antiquity—namely, how the congregations responded to the apostle. In any event, preachers today are very much in the Pauline school by bringing Paul's letters into conversation with the community.

In this regard, many theologians increasingly speak of "traditioning" rather than "tradition." Noting that the Latin verb *traditio* means "to pass on" or "to tradition," the emphasis is on tradition less as a noun (a fixed deposit of ideas and practices) and more as a verb (that is with an emphasis on sorting through how the thoughts and actions of the past can help the community today make its way faithfully through the present). Consequently, many preachers today also speak of Christian "traditioning" rather than simply "tradition." Indeed, without drifting into anachronism, we can view the Bible as not a singular tradition but as a record of different conversations (traditioning) carried on by the Elohists, Yahwists, Deuteronomists, priestly theologians, apocalypticists (including the early Christian writers), and Hellenistic Jewish writers. After the biblical period, the diverse voices in the traditioning conversation are even more apparent—for example, the Cappadocians, Origen, Augustine, Pelagius, Abelard, Catherine of Sienna, Hildegard of Bingen, Thomas Aquinas, Dame Julian of Norwich, the Reformers (and the differences among them), the mystics, and more recently Pentecostals, evangelicals, neo-orthodox, liberation theologians, womanists, feminists, mujeristas, postliberals, and revisionary theologians.

A conversational homiletic simply brings into the open and makes available for critical reflection processes of traditioning that are carried out in communities of the faithful in every era: bringing voices from the past into conversation with one another and with voices in the current setting to identify elements that are instructive and those that need to be adapted for the community to respond as fully as possible to God's gracious presence and leading.

In the deepest sense, a conversational mode of preaching is biblical because it aims to help us do for our moment in history what the biblical writers attempted to do in their times: bring together voices from past and present in artful interchange in search of a vision of God that is faithful, contemporary, liberating, and empowering. This book helps the preacher develop such conversations Sunday by Sunday and season by season.

Ronald J. Allen
Nettie Sweeney and Hugh Th. Miller
Professor of Preaching and New Testament
Christian Theological Seminary

Introduction

I was on the campus of Northwestern University for a conference a few years ago and saw the Alice Millar Chapel for the first time when I and others at the conference attended Sunday morning worship. I arrived for the worship service early, so I had plenty of time to take in my surroundings.

While the chapel is, for the most part, traditionally Gothic, the stained-glass windows are another story altogether. When I looked around at the windows, a jumble of images jumped out at me. There were crosses, a dove, bread and wine, the tablets of the Ten Commandments, the Lamb of God, Noah's ark, angels, the hand of God, icons of the four evangelists . . . images you would expect. But then I also saw a telephone, a tractor, a skeleton, a jellyfish, an astronaut, the U.S. Capital, a railroad crossing, the atom. . . .

The disconnect between the traditional structure and the odd, contemporary images puzzled and overwhelmed me—and caused me no little anxiety. At first I tried to dismiss the windows as just plain unappealing and inappropriate. But the longer I sat there staring at one and then another, the more I sensed that all of these images were connected—or at least could be connected. I started to notice, for instance, that while each individual window is a collage of traditional and nontraditional images, patterns and color schemes run through the whole set of windows.

As numbers in the pews began to grow, regular attendees noticed us visitors staring at the windows with our mouths ajar—a sight they must see every time visitors join the community on Sunday. It didn't take long for a couple of these regular worshipers to ask me, "What do you think of our windows?" and to point out images I hadn't yet found. "Why is that image there?" I asked. "I don't know," would begin the answer, followed by, "but to me it sort of means. . . ."

Thanks to this initial conversation, I began making a little sense of the windows by the end of the service. And, I was delighted when it was announced that the chaplain would be giving a tour of the chapel after worship for those of us attending the conference. I was excited that the mysterious windows would be interpreted once and for all. As he showed us around the sanctuary, the chaplain explained something of the history of the windows. He told how a committee chose themes for the windows that represented the varieties of work of the university—commerce, space, communication, the state, the races of humanity, healing, law, discovery, literature, and the arts. The artist, he explained, chose not to use traditional stained-glass iconography but instead used highly stylized images from the university's themes superimposed upon biblical images in such a way that there is no focal point, no picture depicting a scene, but a collage of clashing images that *require* interpretation and integration by the observer if they are to be meaningful. In the end, however, the chaplain himself, although clearly someone who had studied these windows in great depth, offered no final interpretation of the windows. Instead, he simply complemented the conversation we were already having about the windows by giving us some tools to grapple with the imagery on our own and with one another.

He closed his tour with the story of the controversy that arose when the window committee first saw the artist's plans. Everyone on the committee was taken aback by the proposal, but one member was especially aghast and fought tooth and nail to keep the windows from being installed. He clearly had lost the battle. Now, after worshiping with those windows for over three decades, every so often he comes up to the chaplain and says something like "I was wrong about these windows. I can't imagine church without them. I can't imagine engaging the meaning of the world any other way." And I assume that whenever he spots a visitor sitting in the pews staring at the windows, he sits down with them and asks as I was asked, "What do you think of our windows?" and a new person is drawn into the ongoing, interpretative conversation.

In this book, I propose an approach to the proclamation and preaching of the church that is much like my experience of the multilayered conversations concerning those stained-glass windows. The material is divided into two parts: the first, descriptive, and the second, application.

Part 1 is divided into four chapters. In chapter 1, I offer an overview of the postmodern situation in which individuals make meaning in conversation with a wide variety of truth claims. I then review previous homiletical literature that uses conversation as a model and a method for preaching in this context. In chapter 2, I build on the strengths of these earlier homiletical approaches to develop a theology of proclamation that is rooted in an ecclesiology that views the church as a community of theological conversation, in which individuals gather to proclaim their experiences and interpretations of God, self, and the world in a give-and-take process of making meaning. Chapter 3 presents a theology of preaching as a subcategory of a theology of proclamation. Here I propose that the preacher should not be seen as *the one* in the congregation whom God has called and empowered to proclaim the gospel but as one conversation partner among many in the congregation. As the conversation partner who specializes in the study of Scripture and tradition, the preacher funds the community's meaning-making conversations by providing much of the Christian "language" that is used in the give-and-take proclamation taking place throughout the congregation. Chapter 4 moves from the theological to the practical, exploring the impact of this theology of preaching on the actual work of preparing and offering monological sermons in a conversational congregation. Here the emphasis shifts from the individual sermon as event (the focus of most homiletical literature) to preaching week in and week out to increase the vocabulary of the faith used in the constantly evolving congregational conversation.

In part 2, I demonstrate how this proposal works with a case study of the process of preparing and preaching sermons for an entire liturgical season in the context of a particular conversational community of faith. Many homiletical texts propose a preparation process but few actually walk readers through with enough detail for them to make it their own. Because the process of preparing a number of sermons at the same time is central to this conversational approach, I have decided to illustrate such a process in detail.

Clergy, homileticians, theologians, and laity all recognize that the late twentieth century and the early twenty-first century is a time of significant change. It is not yet clear how the relevancy of the gospel will be claimed and proclaimed in the future. And it is not my intention that this book be seen as offering *the* answer to that question. Instead, I hope that what follows is a helpful contribution to the conversation as the church strives to ask the world, "What do you think of our windows?"

Part 1

A Conversational Homiletic

Chapter 1

Sermons and Conversation

> In the twenty-first century I look forward not to more modernity, or postmodernity, but to a sense of being a part of a new conversation.
> —Theodore Zeldin[1]

I remember off-handedly commenting to a professor some years ago that I thought postmodern concerns were limited to the scholarly and artistic elite. His response was a knowing smirk. Looking back now over my years in parish and campus ministry, I know exactly what that smirk meant, and I realize just how naïve and ignorant I was to think that postmodernism was simply an academic fad. As a college chaplain I worked with an evangelical Baptist student who had folded the idea of karma into his Christian worldview and a Hindu student who quoted from the Gospel of Matthew in every e-mail she sent. And indeed, in one parish an older member would claim in Bible study discussions with one breath, "God said it, I believe it, and that settles it for me," and in the next breath say, "Well, that may be what the Bible means to you, but this is what it means to me. . . ." These kinds of encounters with young and old have led me, as someone who cares about the future of the church and specifically about the future of preaching, to take postmodernism very seriously.

"Postmodernism" is a buzzword used in many different ways by many different people and rejected by many others.[2] References to the postmodern situation pervade recent homiletical literature as well, just as they do literature in all the theological disciplines. My interest is in neither the label nor the academic philosophical discussions of postmodernism per se. I do not catalogue and analyze in detail the various aspects of postmodernism in this book. As someone concerned about how the church goes about the task of proclaiming the good news of Jesus Christ in the early twenty-first century, my interest is concentrated on what Ronald J. Allen calls "folk postmodernism"[3] and what Paul Lakeland refers to as "cultural postmodernism."[4] Specifically, I am inviting us to struggle with the question of the role of preaching in the context of the rejection of Enlightenment epistemology in North American culture.

In the modern Enlightenment worldview, truth is understood as absolute and universal. If it is true here and now, it is true everywhere and always. Moreover, with the rise of the scientific method and the success of science in explaining much of the natural world, reason is given the highest respect in the process of discerning such universal truth. In contrast to premodern, pre-Enlightenment epistemology, truth is no longer seen as divinely revealed from on high but is, rather, objectively discovered from below.

In our day of cultural postmodernism, however, this Enlightenment approach to the world has been overturned . . . to some degree. We shouldn't view this as a conscious, wholesale rejection of Enlightenment epistemology, but it is a serious shift nevertheless. More and more, people in Western culture view truth as particular, local, and thus relative, often without even realizing it; they are comfortable with multiple truths, with competing truths. This sort of approach to truth involves a shift in emphasis from an objective, scientific approach to the world to a subjective encounter with the world. Reason is no longer the sole authority for determining truth. It has been coupled with and limited by individual and communal experience, thus stripping the power from any grand narrative (be it mythic, theological, or scientific) to define the worldview of all.[5]

To borrow Sharon Parks's words, citizens of the postmodern world are less concerned with the task of looking for meaning and are more about the task of "making meaning."[6] This may seem to be a subtle shift in semantics, but it is significant. For a long time the universal question was, "What is the meaning of life?" To some degree that question was replaced in modern times with "What is the meaning of *my* life?" Now many ask, "Is there *any* meaning to life?" And the postmodern answer that individuals often give to this question is, "The only meaning in life is the meaning I *make* of *my* life. Out of my experience with the world, I create meaning and determine what is meaningful." Although postmodernism rejects metanarratives as authoritative *for all*, individuals (and at times groups) work to construct cohesive worldviews for themselves. Those who construct such cohesive worldviews simply consider them to be neither authoritative for nor verifiable by others.

Whether we who stand in the pulpit Sunday after Sunday appreciate or agree with this move toward local worldviews doesn't really matter in the end. The church must take this sort of postmodern approach to meaning seriously because it is so pervasive and because with that view comes a suspicion and distrust of institutions like the church that have traditionally made universal truth claims. Although in the twentieth century a great deal of energy in fundamentalist pulpits was spent defending the traditional faith against scientific claims, much of mainline Protestant preaching embraced the Enlightenment worldview and focused on making the faith reasonable in light of universal truths discovered about the world through the faculty of reason. Preachers attempted to translate the classic symbols and Scriptures of Christianity in a way that allowed modern people who approached the world through the scientific method to accept the faith as rational and useful. Preachers used critical exegetical, historical, and theological methods to offer sermons that would help their congregation maintain a unified worldview in which conflicts between truth claims could be resolved.

But what is the church, which is grounded in the story of Israel and Jesus Christ, to do in a day when grand truth narratives are rejected? How can we speak of creation and exodus and prophecy and incarnation and resurrection and eschaton in a day when truth is considered relative to context and when institutions that want to say more evoke side-glances of suspicion? How is the church to proclaim the gospel when those in the pews are likely to be suspicious of any authoritative claims preachers (or anyone else) make? How are we to preach to a gathering of hearers who are not seeking meaning from us, but are at best going about the task of making meaning for themselves and who approach the Christian faith and what preachers have to say about and from it as one resource among many?

Preachers could, of course, take a stance against postmodernism that leads to an evangelistic approach in the hope of converting our listeners from relative wandering to standing firm on the universal truth of the gospel.[7] To do so, however, is to risk going the hegemonic route of fundamentalism in the modern period and traveling backwards in time instead of responding to the present and participating in the shaping of the future.

I think that an approach is called for that allows preachers both to remain faithful to the ancient Christian traditions and to embrace postmodern congregations. Some homileticians have turned to conversation to do this.[8] While many scholars have described preaching in terms of dialogue or conversation, more often than not these references serve simply as passing metaphors and do not play a major role in their theology or methods for preaching.[9] A handful of recent homileticians, however, have explored conversational models of preaching in some depth to deal with issues of epistemology and authority. Their approaches can be grouped into three categories: conversation during the sermon, conversation before the sermon, and conversational sermons.[10] We will review them briefly to demonstrate the important contributions they have made to homiletical theory and to set the stage for a fourth approach that I will propose.

Conversation during the Sermon

In the 1960s and early 1970s, many viewed preaching as doomed. Some attempts to revive it included experiments in which a monologue sermon was replaced with dialogues in worship.[11] These dialogues usually occurred between two or three "preachers" in front of the congregation or between a preacher and the congregation themselves. The dialogue sermon between preachers was usually a scripted discourse that might have had the appearance of conversation but in reality was a monologue in two voices. This approach lacked the true give-and-take nature of conversation and kept the congregation in the passive role of observers. The dialogue sermons between pastor and congregation, while not monologue in disguise, were little better. Except in a very small congregation, the time allotted for the sermon within the worship service rarely allowed for the intimate evolution of ideas and emotions that occurs in authentic conversations between two or more people. Moreover, the preacher remained at the authoritative center of the dialogue as individuals in the congregation talked to her or him instead of truly being in conversation with one another. These early attempts at dialogue sermons represent more of a worship gimmick than a true paradigm shift in the church's approach to proclamation.

In the 1980s, Bernard J. Lee suggested a new approach to a "shared homily" with the intent of avoiding the freewheeling sharing of unreflective understandings that occurred in most dialogue sermons.[12] Lee used Gadamer's and Ricoeur's hermeneutics to imagine how groups of five to fifteen Christians would enter into risky conversation with the biblical text and with one another. He identified three structured conversational moments: 1) sharing initial understandings of the text, 2) hearing the text on its own ground (as offered by a minister of the Word), and 3) sharing new responses to the text. While Lee's disciplined mode of conversation offers much to the idea of group Bible studies, it falls victim to some of the same problems that plagued earlier approaches to dialogue preaching. Because the process requires small groups, normal worship with a congregation larger than fifteen requires choosing between two less than perfect options. In one approach, the congregation can be divided into groups with different facilitators. This approach results, however, in a loss of the sense of community of the whole congregation that is created by the rest of the liturgy. In the second approach, a representative group from the congregation has the disciplined conversation in front of the rest of those gathered to worship. While this avoids the scripted quality of dialogue preachers, it nevertheless pushes most of the congregation back into the role of passive observers.

Lee's interest in fostering deeper engagement between the text and the congregation as well as between members of the congregation is a move in the right direction, and his conversational approach has much to offer other settings within the life of the congregation that allow for greater intimacy and more extended commitments of time to the conversation.[13] Incorporating the style of conversation he suggests into liturgical settings, however, does not eliminate the problems of the 1960s dialogue sermons that he criticizes.

Conversation before the Sermon

In another homiletical approach the preacher and the congregation engage communally in conversation as part of the preacher's process of sermon preparation. The result is a monological sermon that has some qualities of being a collaborative product of clergy and laity. This approach has been supported by a number of scholars and preachers.

The first proposal for this sort of communal approach seems to have come not from a homiletician but from a theologian. Dietrich Ritschl, in his neorthodox *A Theology of Preaching*, argues that the whole church, not just the preacher, participates in the office of proclamation.[14] Although it is difficult to gather many members of the congregation who take this responsibility seriously, Ritschl argues that preachers should engage a circle of members of the congregation with whom they listen to the Word before preaching it. This does not mean that, in the end, the church preaches the sermon to itself. Ritschl proposes that cooperative sermon preparation be limited to the early stages of work. The final stages of preparation and certainly the sermon delivery must be left to the preacher, but he carries this responsibility differently having started out the process in community.

In *Parish Back Talk*, Browne Barr offered a brief description of a "sermon seminar" approach to conversations preceding the Sunday sermon similar to Ritschl's proposal in that it combines communal conversations with individual pastoral authority.[15] Barr's proposal, however, grows out of practical experience in his California parish rather than theology. The process he proposes works as follows: The entire congregation is invited to a mid-week discussion of the biblical text that will be the focus of the Sunday sermon. The preacher for the coming Sunday opens with a brief, nontechnical exegesis of the passage. Then the crowd divides into groups of eight to ten for a forty-minute discussion of the text. These discussions are not tightly structured, but the groups are instructed to "follow the lead of the scripture" while also paying attention to "their own problems and questions of faith and life." After the group discussions, the crowd reassembles and each group makes a brief report about their conversation. The evening ends with fifteen or so minutes of prayer that grows out of the conversation with and about the biblical passage. Barr argues that these discussions often lead to a place where the preacher had no suspicion he or she might go with the sermon. Indeed, on Sunday, a great deal of the sermon that the preacher delivers will be composed of interpretive observations and illustrations offered by those participating in the seminar.[16]

Although other scholars have also advocated for such a collaborative approach to sermon development,[17] it is John S. McClure who has most recently and most thoroughly reintroduced and developed the pre-sermon discussion process. In his 1995 work, *The Roundtable Pulpit: Where Leadership and Preaching Meet*, McClure argues for collaborative leadership styles for pastors that incorporate both integrative power (in which leaders form power alliances that benefit all members of the community) and nutritive power (in which leaders invite others to assume responsibility for the direction of their own lives and assume leadership roles themselves).[18] In such a form of shared leadership, the preacher does not have to abandon a charismatic form of authority in the pulpit but instead can complement it by serving as "host" to all in the community who have a word to share. The preacher must, however, abandon a sovereign homiletic in which she or he stands above the congregation in a hierarchical, authoritarian relationship and offers the sermon as mandate. Moreover, the preacher must also move beyond dialogue, narrative, and inductive modes of preaching, which do attempt to address the hierarchical problems of sovereign preaching by attending to the experience of the hearers but nevertheless assume that there is a symmetry of experience shared by preacher and hearer that can preclude the otherness of the hearers.

What is called for, therefore, is a collaborative homiletic in which preacher and hearers engage in a structured conversation as part of the process of sermon preparation. Instead of looking for theological consensus or symmetry of experience, the sermon roundtable that McClure proposes is a learning community that values difference as the very thing that creates a conversation from which a transforming word emerges. In this model, the preacher and another congregational leader serve as cohosts of this sermon roundtable, which consists of a maximum of ten members who are listed in the worship bulletin. Membership should reflect the diversity of the congregation and its regular visitors as well as members of the church staff, and should change regularly to bring different voices into the pulpit.[19] The group should meet once a week for ninety minutes with the following sort of structure:

> 10 minutes—Cohost asks how the previous Sunday's sermon reflected or failed to reflect the group's conversation and what feedback they heard about the sermon.

> 20 minutes—Cohost leads a discussion in which the group engages the biblical text in an exegetical discussion. The preacher may serve as a resource in this discussion as one who has studied the historical and literary background of the passage.

> 60 minutes—Cohost helps the group lift their heads out of the text and engage one another based on their encounter of the text. The group sets topics for the conversation; interprets the meaning of these topics for their lives, the church, and the world; empowers those who have not spoken to share feelings and thoughts; comes to terms with what the gospel (as explored in the conversation) requires of individuals and of the church; and discusses how to fulfill those requirements.

At the end of this process, the preacher is free to build on the conversation using his or her own theological, biblical, and cultural interpretation. It is not the job of the preacher, who has listened to and participated in the conversation, to step into the pulpit and simply give a report on the conversation in the role of a recording secretary. Even as the preacher takes creative license in creating the sermon, however, she or he must strive to be true to the *dynamics* of the roundtable conversation. Being true to these dynamics will include describing elements of the conversation at times and at other times imitating those elements. The end result is not a sermon shaped by a lone-ranger exegete, but an offering from the congregation through the preacher (who is part of the congregation) to the congregation.

There is much to commend McClure's collaborative approach. Like Bernard Lee's model, it involves true conversation. Moving the conversation to a time before the sermon, however, allows for more intimacy and depth than did incorporating it into the worship service itself. Likewise, the setting and approach McClure proposes values and highlights difference of experience and beliefs in the community of faith. And, indeed, the role of the preacher shifts from an authority figure who declares truth from above to one who comes out from the congregation to proclaim the gospel by representing the dynamics of a conversation held by representatives of the congregation. At the same time, the preacher is not without authority. She or he has chosen the scriptural text for the sermon (thus determining the beginning and scope of the conversation) and shapes the final monological sermon alone, choosing how to represent the dynamics of the conversation by deciding which voices will echo forward to Sunday worship and which will grow silent. In some sense, what McClure has done is to supplement inductive preaching with a pre-sermon group process. Whereas Fred Craddock (whom McClure discusses) argues that the preacher's task in the pulpit is to represent the *experience* of the gospel she or he has in the study through the exegetical process,[20] McClure argues that the preacher is to represent the *dynamics* (i.e., group experience) of the exegetical conversation. Nevertheless, if the sermon is to be retained as a monologue that grows out of a collaborative exegetical effort, this balance between the individual authority of the preacher and the responsibility of the preacher to her or his conversation partners seems a pretty good one.

The primary problem with McClure's proposal is that the conversation is narrowly defined as being in service to the proclamation of the gospel that occurs in the Sunday sermon service. Is not the conversation itself proclamation? Assuming that this is the case, the emphasis in a conversational homiletic should be shifted away from the sermon and onto the conversation itself. In other words, a true conversational homiletic should ultimately view the sermon as being in service to the congregation's proclamation-conversations instead of the congregation's conversation being in service to the preacher's sermon.

Conversational Sermons

In the midst of the worship crisis and experimentation with dialogue sermons that arose in the 1960s and 1970s, Reuel Howe published *Partners in Preaching: Clergy and Laity in Dialogue.*[21] Howe's proposal differs from experimental approaches that use dialogue as a method in worship in that he invites his readers to consider a dialogical *principle* for monological preaching.

As an agent enabling the dialogue between God and the worshiper, the preacher seeks to preach in a way that brings contemporary life and tradition into conversation with one another in the sermon, so that an exchange can take place between the meanings the listeners bring from their lives and experiences and the meanings of the gospel. In other words, the sermon invites the hearers to create their own conversation between the secular and the religious. The goal of the preacher's sermon, therefore, is not to interpret and apply the gospel in such a fashion that it is the final word for all gathered but to give birth to sermons brought into being by the individual members of the congregation. This should lead, in turn, to the laity continuing the church's sermon as they disperse to dialogue with and act in the secular world.

What Howe referred to in the 1960s as a homiletical principle, George Swank labeled a preaching *style* in the early 1980s. In *Dialogical Style in Preaching*, Swank combined Howe's dialogical principle with the inductive approach to preaching introduced by Fred Craddock.[22] Swank proposed that a dialogical sermon begins with the preacher listening to the people before ever stepping into the pulpit. He or she then crafts a sermon that relates to questions they have raised and concerns they have shared. This sermon should be open-ended and invite each listener to reflect inwardly in such a way that she or he creates a self-tailored message that is more intimate and effective than any message the preacher could offer.

Such a sermon is not a possession of the preacher but of the church. The preacher simply creates an inductive sermon that encourages the people to "sermonize" within themselves. The assumption behind this style of preaching is that the people do not need the preacher to tell them what they ought to believe. Through the guidance of the Holy Spirit, they are able to test thoughts, draw Christian conclusions, and discern God's will for themselves. The sermon does not make sense of the universe for the listeners but is the catalyst for them to do that which they have had the capacity to do all along.

In the mid-1990s, Lucy Atkinson Rose, in *Sharing the Word: Preaching in the Roundtable Church*, revised this conversational theology of preaching by offering a feminist approach to postmodern questions about the authority of the preacher and the relative nature of truth.[23] She begins by reviewing and evaluating three broad theories of preaching that have dominated twentieth-century homiletics. The first is "traditional homiletical theory" as found in the classic and popular homiletical textbook written by John A. Broadus in 1870 and revised by Jesse Burton Weatherspoon in 1944.[24] In this model, the goal of preaching is to persuade the hearers of the truth of the message being transmitted. This goal presupposes a gap between the preacher (as the sender of communication) and the congregation (as recipients). For Rose, this theory is problematic in that a hierarchical relationship between the preacher and the congregation is the foundation of the preaching moment: the congregation sits passively below while the preacher stands above declaring absolute truth.

The second theory is the "kerygmatic theory" that grows out of the influence of C. H. Dodd's attempt to identify the original content of the apostolic proclamation[25] and Karl Barth's theology of the preacher as a "herald" through whom God speaks in the sermon event to reveal the Word.[26] This approach is also problematic in that the hierarchical gap between preacher and congregation is widened since 1) the preacher's words are to be identified with God's words and 2) the sermon offers the gospel's essential kernel, which communicates and effects salvation.

Rose labels the third theory (or group of theories) that she reviews "transformational" and includes in the category those scholars usually associated with the "New Homiletic." Rose's label identifies the purpose of the sermon in these models as being the facilitation of an experience that changes individual's values, worldviews, or reality. Here the influence is not neoorthodoxy but the existentialist theology and hermeneutics of Rudolf Bultmann and Paul Tillich. While it would seem that the gap between the preacher and the congregation is reduced by defining the preacher as one who shapes an experience for the congregation by attending to their world and needs rather than a vessel for God's truth, the gap remains, for the preacher retains the privileged position of already possessing the authentic experience of transformation that she or he now offers to the hearers.

Rose, attempting to build on the strengths and correct some of the weaknesses of these earlier theories, proposes a conversational approach to preaching. The purpose of preaching in this model is to gather the community of faith, week after week, around the Word where the central conversations of the church are refocused and fostered. The gap between preacher and congregation is reduced by the preacher standing in solidarity with the congregation exploring together the mystery of the Word for their own lives, as well as the life of the congregation, the larger church, and the world. Rose properly locates the gap between the community of faith (including both preacher and congregation) on the one hand and a text, meaning, or mystery on the other. This means that instead of persuading the hearers to accept a truth, offering the hearers kerygmatic salvation, or mediating a transforming experience of the gospel, conversational preachers, out of the depths of their convictions and experiences, propose a tentative interpretation of Scripture and of life to the congregation for their additions, corrections, or counterproposals. The language of the sermon, therefore, must be confessional, reflecting the accumulated and ongoing experiences of the people of God, and must be evocative, empowering the generation of multiple meanings.

Ronald J. Allen also proposes conversational sermons. To my knowledge, Allen is the only scholar to use the concept of conversational sermons in a significant fashion in an introductory homiletical textbook.[27] He has argued that the sermon is a conversation in which the congregation, preacher, and others search for an adequate theological interpretation of life and the world.[28] While still a monologue, says Allen, a sermon can have the qualities of a vibrant family conversation around the dinner table. Indeed, in line with the use of conversation as a metaphor in hermeneutics and theology, he views the preaching conversation as involving not people alone but also the Bible, Christian history and tradition, contemporary theologians, the congregation, the wider world, the life experience of the preacher, and God.[29] As the preacher develops and embodies a sermon, she or he asks of each of these partners, What do you ask us to believe is true of God, what do you ask us to accept as God's purposes for the world, and what do you ask us to do?

For Allen, the conversation among these partners is structured by the sermonic goal of mutual critical correlation between the claims of ancient Christian traditions and the present social-intellectual-theological situation.[30] But this correlation is not a straightforward application of past answers to today's questions. The interchange with multiple conversation partners requires also the critique of the tradition from the perspective of contemporary insights and the constant reevaluation and reformulation of aspects of the contemporary church's interpretation of the gospel. The criteria Allen suggests for shaping this mutual critical correlating conversation are borrowed from theologian Clark Williamson: appropriateness to the gospel, intelligibility, and moral plausibility.[31]

The particular sermon that results from this conversational process does not represent an end to the conversation. The sermon is a mile-marker of the interpretation of the gospel at and for a particular moment in history. At best, the interpretation is a "relatively adequate witness" to the gospel, an interpretation that should be revisited and rethought by the preacher and the congregation from the perspective of fresher insights at other times.

While Rose's and Allen's proposals are by no means identical, they have similarities, and indeed their understandings of conversational sermons offer much to those wishing to preach authentically in a postmodern culture. The tentative and open-ended quality of conversational preachers' interpretations funds hearers' (and preachers') struggles to make meaning of their lives and of the world in a less hierarchical fashion than earlier theories of preaching. However, the conversation happens more fully for the preacher than it does for the congregation. In fact, it is not clear that the congregation ever actually engages in *real* conversations in this model. At best the conversation may happen for individuals in the congregation who use the sermon to fund an interior conversation.

Moreover, in both Rose's and Allen's proposals the sermon is the *starting* point of any conversation that does continue after the sermon. Even though they both propose *tentative* interpretations of Scripture as the goal of the sermon, these tentative interpretations are the focus of any follow-up questions, corrections, or counterproposals. Indeed, one is given the impression that without the sermon, the church would have no conversations at all. It should be the other way around. Without conversations in the church where the congregation is struggling to proclaim the gospel already, there is no occasion at all for a sermon. Moreover, if the emphasis in a true conversational homiletic is on the ongoing conversations in the church, preachers must focus more on how preaching week after week, year after year, participates in these conversations instead of focusing so much on the individual sermon as the occasion for the conversation.[32]

Preaching in a Conversational Church

These three approaches to integrating conversation and proclamation— conversation during the sermon, conversation before the sermon, and conversational sermons—have greatly enriched the homiletical discussion concerning the purpose and practice of preaching. Moreover, I am personally more in debt to the work of the scholars reviewed here than I can express. While I have taken issue with individual elements of their proposals in order to clear ground for my own, in reality my proposal is more an extension of their work than a radical turn in a new direction.

It seems to me that the most appropriate way to extend their work is to begin by shifting the locus of the conversation from the preacher and the sermon to the congregation itself. By moving the conversational furniture of the church around in this manner, the sermon is in service to the proclamatory conversation instead of vice versa. And the sermon ceases to be the starting point or the center of the conversation and becomes a significant contributing factor to the ongoing conversations owned by the community. Indeed, a true conversational homiletic should begin with the recognition that the proclamation of the gospel is a shared responsibility of the church offered through a matrix of theological, religious, political, and personal conversations, not solely the duty of the preacher standing alone in the pulpit. I turn to this beginning now.

Chapter 2

A Conversational Ecclesiology

Let two or three prophets speak, and let the others weigh what is said. If a revelation is made to someone sitting nearby, let the first person be silent. For you all can prophesy one by one, so that all may learn and all be encouraged.

—1 Corinthians 14:29–31

My particular approach to a conversational homiletic is rooted in 1) a view of the church as a community of theological, political, historical, spiritual, ritual, and existential conversation and 2) a view of preaching in which the pulpit is placed on the edge of the community's conversational circle and the preacher's is one voice among many in a matrix of congregational conversations. The monological preaching is, of course, dependent on the communal proclamation. Therefore, before we can explore and develop the theology of preaching I wish to propose, we must first explore and develop a conversational ecclesiology.

This approach is a significant shift from standard operating procedure in homiletics. As L. Susan Bond notes, "Ecclesiology, or the nature of the church, is not always an immediate consideration for homiletical theorists. Homileticians tend to think first of the nature of sermonic content (whether theological or biblical content) and how that content will best be offered for the hearers." She presses the point further by claiming, "Even though homiletical theory almost always assumes something about the greater purposes of the church, relatively little attention has been given to the relationship between homiletical theory and the broader corporate vocation or identity of the community of believers."[1] While I hope to deal with this deficiency by understanding a theology of preaching as a subcategory of an ecclesiological approach to proclamation, I must state from the outset that the ecclesiological reflections I offer in this chapter are not meant in any way to describe the totality of the church's life and mission. They are intentionally narrow and suggestive rather than exhaustive and systematic. Nevertheless, they will ground our homiletic for these postmodern times.

The Church as a Community of Conversation

As I noted in chapter 1, people who share postmodern approaches to the world make meaning for themselves by picking and choosing from a wide variety of sources of knowledge. Drawing from popular expressions of different faith traditions, educational opportunities, art, others' personal narratives, politics, news media, the entertainment and marketing industries, face-to-face discussions, on-line correspondence, and so forth, they construct that which they hold to be of Ultimate Concern (to use Paul Tillich's phrase) without claiming that any of their sources of knowledge or their particular construction of reality holds absolute truth for all. Although in this culture of folk postmodernism, individuals may still attempt to develop unified, comprehensive worldviews, there is no universally accepted metanarrative to which they hold complete allegiance, to which they expect others to be completely loyal, or by which they comprehensively test competing truth claims. What they hold to be ultimate, they do not claim to be absolute for all. Different postmodern people give different weight to different sources of knowledge, and they are comfortable with all of this difference.

In other words, citizens of the postmodern culture *make* meaning in a conversational manner, giving and taking from the myriad of "conversation" partners we have in today's world. Indeed, hardly a waking moment passes when we don't encounter implicit claims about meaning in today's world. We wake up to the clock radio and go to sleep with the TV on. We surf the Internet, skim the newspaper, and devour the gossip tabloids. We chat with neighbors and debate with coworkers. And we are constantly bombarded by advertising. In this kind of existence, people make meaning cafeteria-style, picking and choosing what they wish from all these different conversation partners and leaving much that is unappealing to them for others to consume.

It seems pretty straightforward that if church talk wants to play a more significant role in funding the meaning-making process of members of our postmodern society, it will require more than bringing conversation into worship. It will also require more than having broader and more frequent conversations about sermons or having preachers step out of high pulpits and stand at floor level to offer conversational sermons. There needs to be more conscious, theologically oriented conversation *throughout* the congregation—more *circles* of conversation in which church talk seriously engages all of the other conversations going on in our culture as people try to make meaning in a relative yet global context.[2]

In other words, the church needs a new theology of and approach to proclamation, in which all members of the congregation are seen not only as recipients of the church's proclamation but also providers of it. All people who struggle with the Christian faith are called on to proclaim the gospel to one another in a give-and-take fashion.[3]

Since the time of Luther, the metaphor "Word of God" has been reserved for Christ, the Bible, and preaching. But this has equated the preacher's voice with Christ's and the Bible, and that is a false equation, at least in the sense that the preacher's voice *alone* is to be equated with these. Other forms of proclamation practiced by the church (e.g., music, art, social action, charity, prayer, Sunday school, higher educational institutions, and missions) are seen as being subordinate to and originating in the proclamation that occurs in the pulpit. At best, such a view places the laity as mediators, standing between the ordained preacher and the world. They are reduced to the role of dealers in second-hand proclamation.

To reserve for the ordained preacher the right and responsibility to proclaim Christ, however, distorts a biblical view of the community as a composite of baptized persons endowed with a range of spiritual gifts that are to be used for the building up of the church, its members, and the world in which the church resides. In reality, the church and its members proclaim the gospel in a myriad of ways. Preaching is but one method of proclamation, standing alongside (not above) all of the other methods.

A better understanding of God's gifts of proclamation is that proclamation flows out of the central act of the church's witness. Although there are many sides to and many aspects of the mission of the church, the central act of the church's witness is simply the *gathering* of the community as the body of Christ. After all, the New Testament term for the church is just that—gathering, assembly (*ekklesia*). If proclamation (as well as all other forms of the church's mission) flows out of the act of gathering, then it flows *through* everyone who gathers. And if everyone is proclaiming, then the emphasis in a theology of proclamation shifts from a monological funnel (from Christ through the Bible through the preacher to the congregation and to the world) to a conversational ecclesiology in which the gospel moves back and forth among the gathered community in the form of statements and questions and in the form of yes and no. In other words, the priesthood of all believers should include a *homiletic of all believers*. To borrow a phrase from Rebecca Chopp, "The *community* is the manifestation of Word for the world."[4] Through proclamatory conversations that occur within the church and between the church and the world (of which the church is part and parcel), all participants in the church are continually and simultaneously offering and receiving the good news of Jesus Christ.[5]

Churches that continue to dictate truth authoritatively from above in a world where meaning is more and more constructed experientially from below are doomed to a future of speaking only to those who turn to and hold on to the historic faith primarily out of fear of the ambiguities of postmodern relativity. The authority to describe God, to explore the human condition and God's response to it, and to declare what it means to be Christian (individually) and the church (communally) in the world must be shifted out of the mouth of the preacher and into mouths of the community of faith as a whole if the Christian faith is to serve as a resource for those struggling to make meaning in today's postmodern culture.

Such a conversational approach is not only appropriate to the nature of postmodern meaning making by individuals, however. It also reflects the historical vocation of the church to be, among other things, a community of theological reflection. John B. Cobb argues that one of the errors that the twenty-first century church must correct is the twentieth-century church's turning over of theology to the university. This professionalization of theology has created a gap between theology and church life (i.e., between reflection and praxis) that leads the church into "decadence."[6] One might say that academic Christian theology has had little to do with defining or being defined by real-life, on-the-streets and in-the-pews Christianity. Conversely, one might also claim that real-life Christianity has had little to do with engaging in serious Christian theology. Cobb argues neither situation should exist and suggests that the solution to this problem is to begin with congregations, not with the academy:

> The renewal of the vocation of theology in the churches will not, and cannot, come from professional theologians whose work centers in academia. It can only come from the churches themselves, which, without such renewal, are condemned to continuing lukewarmness and the resulting decline. This does not mean that pastors and lay

[handwritten marginalia: "I disagree academia must begin it too!"]

[handwritten note at bottom: "How else are pastors going to help their laity if academia doesn't attend to it!"]

people in large numbers must study the writings of academic theologians. It does require that church people recognize that unless we reflect seriously, as Christians, about who we are and what we are called to be, we continue to drift into decadence. It also requires that, instead of being driven to despair by such recognition, we begin the process of reflection involving as many of our people as possible.[7]

As the body of Christ in which all have spiritual gifts (Rom. 12:3–8; 1 Cor. 12) and in which there is neither Jew nor Greek, slave nor free, male nor female (Gal. 3:28), the distinction between laity on the one hand and clergy and academicians on the other must be removed when it comes to the task of *doing* theology and proclaiming the faith. Having a Master of Divinity does not mean one has truly mastered divinity. Being ordained does not make one more closely related to God than others. While important, education and ordination do not grant one deeper perspective into life than others have, do not guarantee one more authentic experiences to be shared than others have, do not insure one more correct views on the nature of the universe than others. The full membership of the church, from youth to the aged, from the poor to the privileged, may not be able to read Mark in the original Greek or recount the debate between Arius and Athanasius or quote Jürgen Moltmann, but they can do theology, and they can, out of their own process of making meaning in and of the world, proclaim their perspective on/from the Christian faith authentically and meaningfully. As sure as they have experienced God (and if God is *everywhere*, then *everyone* has experienced God), then they can participate in give-and-take God-talk. They can proclaim what they experience, think, feel, believe, and interpret to be meaningful at an ultimate level. And what they claim to be meaningful will evolve as they listen to and reflect on the experiences, thoughts, emotions, faith, and interpretations of others. Moreover, as individual participants in the church's conversation grow in this way, the congregational conversation will deepen. In other words, such cooperative theologizing and proclamation will have profound effects not only on postmodern individuals but also on postmodern communities of faith as a whole.

Congregations, therefore, need to engage in thoroughgoing theological conversations if they are 1) to be significant partners to postmodern individuals in their meaning-making endeavors and 2) to reclaim a sense of communal vocation for the church in a world where meaning making is viewed in more and more individualistic terms. So what is the nature of conversation that is suitable and useful for a congregation and its members who are striving to create meaning for their lives and their community as they interpret God, the world, the church, and the self?

The Term "Conversation"

Before we begin to struggle with this question, it is important to determine whether the term "conversation" is the best label for the kind of proclamatory discourse that should define and be fostered throughout the community of faith. After all, there is a wide range of terms available to describe give-and-take speech between people: talk, communication, discussion, chat, discourse, conversation, debate, dialogue, banter, argument. Scholars who investigate such issues primarily use either dialogue or conversation as their primary term for the kind of discussion they are describing. Their preferences for one term over the other usually involve technical definitions and distinctions, such as how formal or informal or how structured or free flowing the discourse is or should be.[8]

In common parlance, of course, conversation and dialogue are nearly synonymous. More important than differences between the two are their similarities when contrasted with two other speech forms—monologue and debate/argument. In monologue, one participant serves as the speaker (implying an active role as giver of speech) and other participants listen (implying a passive role as recipients). In dialogue and conversation, in contrast, all participants potentially take on the roles of both listener and speaker. In give-and-take fashion, all those in a conversation participate in the meaning making of others and invite others to influence their own meaning making.

Conversation and dialogue must also be differentiated from debate and argument. Although debate and argument imply that participants are both speakers and listeners, the goal and nature of the discussion is different from conversation and dialogue in several ways:

- *Dialogue is collaborative: two or more sides work together toward common understanding.* Debate is oppositional: two sides oppose one another and attempt to prove one another wrong.
- *In dialogue, one listens to the other side(s) in order to understand, find meaning, and find agreement.* In debate, one listens to the other side in order to find flaws and to counter its argument.
- *Dialogue enlarges and possibly changes a participant's point of view.* Debate affirms a participant's own point of view.

- *Dialogue reveals assumptions for reevaluation.* Debate defends assumptions as truth.
- *Dialogue creates an open-ended attitude: an openness to being wrong and an openness to change.* Debate creates a close-minded attitude, a determination to be right.
- *Dialogue involves a real concern for the other person and seeks not to alienate or offend.* Debate involves a countering of the other position without focusing on feelings or relationship and often belittles or deprecates the other person.
- *Dialogue remains open-ended.* Debate implies a conclusion.[9]

In sum, the goal of debate and argument is persuasion; one position is accepted and another is not; one person or group wins, and another loses. Of course, there are certainly times in the church's life when debate is necessary and called for; when difficult communal decisions must be made, stances taken, or conflict resolved. Attempts to persuade are important parts of these discussions. But such times should represent unique moments in the ongoing conversations in the life of the church and not the norm. The church's ongoing conversations should set the tone and structure for moments of debate instead of debate setting the tone and structure for the church's ongoing conversations. Imagine how different the church's debates concerning abortion and homosexuality would be if they were informed by dialogues/conversations about such issues, if on both sides attempts at mutual understanding preceded arguments about right and wrong, and if a willingness to test one's own opinions and belief preceded struggles to persuade.

In contrast to moments of debate, the end goal of ongoing theological, proclamatory conversation in the church in general is not persuasion, but *conversion*, in the etymological sense of the word. Indeed, "converse" and "convert" share the same etymological root—the Latin word *convertere*. The prefix *con* means "together" and *vertere* means "to turn." Therefore, speaking etymologically, conversation is "turning together," or mutual conversion.[10] Thus while dialogue and conversation are both to be distinguished from monologue and debate, and while many of the scholars whom I quote in this chapter use the term *dialogue*, I prefer the term *conversation* to name the church's proclamatory discourse, because (as I am using it) it carries with it this understanding of conversion.

The church has always been and should always be concerned with conversion. But in a postmodern era, our understanding of and approach to conversion must change. We usually think of conversion in terms of proselytizing in which one person or group convinces someone outside of the faith to accept their position and become a part of their group. This implies a dramatic and radical intellectual and spiritual life change. But in the etymological sense in which I am using conversion, every time two or more people enter into authentic conversation with one another, they are mutually transformed. At times, the transformations may be dramatic 180-degree reversals, but more often than not they are minute transformations representing a degree or two of turning.[11]

Such minute transformations may not be the ingredients of great altar calls, but the church should value them greatly, since all of the transformations we experience, through all of the conversations in which we participate in life, play an enormous role in how we evolve as persons, how our relationships to God and neighbor grow, and how our understanding of human cultures and of the universe develop—in other words, how we make meaning. Regardless of whether we end our conversation in agreement or not, I am transformed by my conversation with you, you are transformed by your conversation with me, and so on and so forth.[12] In conversation, as we assume the roles of both speakers and listeners, we are give-and-take converters and converted. But, as noted earlier, we should not think only in terms of individual conversions. Every time a group engages in conversation and individuals change, the group changes as well. Conversation in the church creates individual and communal transformation; it creates conversion to the church, within the church, and of the church.

Of course, not all speech between human beings has a positive orientation that promotes well-being and growth (i.e., conversion). As children, we ironically spout the retort, "Sticks and stones may break my bones, but words can never harm me," specifically because we have already felt the sting of an insult. As words can be powerful tools to create, shape, and affirm life and meaning, they can also be powerful tools that cause pain and wreak havoc on others. Speaking etymologically, we could call this improper use of conversation "diversion" instead of conversion, in the sense that it *turns away*, or *turns in different directions*, instead of facilitating a "turning together." Verbal misbehavior such as passive aggressive comments, lies, insults, assertions of power, misrepresentation of facts, and misapplication of the gospel can inflict emotional harm and create distortional views of reality. We know of this side of language from both our personal relationships and from the public sphere of politics and marketing.[13] And, of course, such speech is a part of the church and every congregation's conversational past.[14] So a significant element of our ongoing conversations must include the search for reconciliation and healing within the conversation itself, among its participants and extended to those the church's conversations impact directly and indirectly.

But we must also work to limit the occurrence and effects of such harmful speech in the ecclesial (and secular) conversations of the future. This requires developing some shared principles and disciplines of conversation in the community of faith. Thus we now turn our attention to aspects of proclamatory conversation that should be valued and nurtured by the church.

Appropriate Conversation for the Church

A number of writers concerned with the conversational nature of preaching or other elements of ministry and congregational life have drawn on the description of conversation as it is applied to the hermeneutical situation in the works of Hans-George Gadamer[15] and David Tracy.[16] This is a somewhat awkward move, however. Hermeneutics has taken the term *conversation*, which literally refers to communicative, human exchange, and has applied it metaphorically to the exchange between "text" and "reader." This is a provocative and illuminating way to describe not only how readers interpret texts but also how texts interpret readers. But it is cumbersome and circular to take this metaphorical use and understanding of conversation in hermeneutics and reapply it to the literal exchange between people.[17]

Therefore, in developing my thoughts concerning the nature of conversation appropriate for the church, I have relied on sociological, philosophical, and pedagogical literature that analyzes and promotes the actual use of conversation and dialogue.[18] Since our concern in the next chapter will turn to the role of the preacher in the congregational conversations, I have especially found proposals dealing with pedagogical approaches utilizing conversation and dialogue illuminating.[19] Conversational models that deal with issues of the teacher's role and authority in an educational community that values conversation serve as a helpful albeit imperfect analogy for our starting point for thinking about the church as a community of conversation and the preacher's role in such a community.[20]

Conversational Ethics

The first thing we need to consider in shaping the church's conversations is a sense of the kind of community that is formed in conversational moments, the kind of ethic that shapes the conversational community. After all, as Nicolas Burbules, a specialist in the use of dialogue in the classroom, points out,

> Dialogue is not fundamentally a specific communicative form of question and response, but at heart a kind of *social relation* that engages its participants. A successful dialogue involves a willing partnership and cooperation in the face of likely disagreements, confusions, failures and misunderstandings. Persisting in the process requires a relation of mutual respect, trust, and concern—and part of the dialogical interchange often must relate to the establishment and maintenance of these bonds. The substance of this interpersonal relation is deeper, and more consistent, than any particular communicative form it might take.[21]

For any ecclesial conversation to be an authentic expression of the church's call to be the body of Christ, therefore, a certain amount of *trust* is necessary.[22] The level of trust, of course, deepens as partners sustain a conversational relationship over time.[23] And different types of conversation require different levels of trust and confidentiality. But even at the beginning of a public conversation in the church, there should be a sense that anyone who chooses to gather at the conversational table enters into a covenant of granting a basic level of trust and striving to be trustworthy herself or himself. I should be able to trust that no one in the conversation will either intentionally mislead or injure me or anyone else in the conversation or intentionally misrepresent facts on which their viewpoints are based. Expressed positively, even though I may be meeting conversation partners for the first time, I should be confident that everyone at the table is striving (even if we falter at times) to be honest, respectful, and edifying. When other conversation partners proclaim their experiences, interpretations, and understanding of God and God's creation, I can trust that they are sincere, and they can trust that I, too, am sincere, even when my proclamation disagrees with theirs.[24]

Unlike the hierarchical structuring of community often exhibited in worship and especially in preaching, this kind of trusting, covenantal conversation implies an *egalitarian* view of community, in which all conversation partners are equally valued and all voices are welcome around the table. This egalitarian approach to the conversational community does not mean that everyone gathered is equal in intellectual ability, knowledge of the subject/issues being discussed, life experience, or spiritual wisdom.[25]

Instead, it implies a valuing of persons in the conversation *as persons*. In Paulo Friere's words, "Love is at the same time the foundation of dialogue and dialogue itself. It is thus the task of responsible Subjects and cannot exist in a relation of domination."[26] Or to borrow Martin Buber's well-known phrase, for an ecclesial conversation to be redemptive and effect conversion of all involved, it must be built on I-Thou relationships, in which all participants are valued as mutually edifying Subjects instead of treated as objects of edification.[27] In the case of proclamation, treating others as objects usually implies that they are objects to be filled by a preacher pouring out (i.e., pouring *down*) the Word of God.[28] To value participants in the conversation as Subjects constructs the conversation as a give-and-take partnership among all involved. All are seeking to be filled by others and to offer what they have for the filling of others.[29]

In other words, true conversation demands a golden rule of *reciprocity*. As Burbules says,

> Dialogue is guided by a spirit of discovery, so that the typical tone of a dialogue is exploratory and interrogative. It involves a commitment to the process of communicative exchange itself, a willingness to 'see things through' to some meaningful understandings or agreements among the participants. Furthermore, it manifests an attitude of reciprocity among the participants: an interest, respect, and concern that they share for one another, even in the face of disagreements. . . .[30]

At its most basic level, this reciprocity means that I claim the right to speak not only for myself but for everyone else at the table as well. And when I speak I should be able to trust that I will be listened to and taken seriously just as, when others speak, I listen to and take their words seriously.

This rule does not dictate, however, that everyone must consent to whatever one lays upon the conversational table. *Asymmetry*—difference in beliefs, commitments, and experience—is essential to conversation and should be highly valued.[31] Any conversation partner may disagree with me and should indeed express that disagreement.[32] But as they do that, they will still show respect for me as a person and will not caricature or belittle my experiences, ideas, and beliefs. Moreover, before immediately jumping to disagreement and debate, they open themselves to what I have to offer. In other words, they are willing to risk changing their minds and altering their beliefs (i.e., being converted) by whatever I or anyone else in the conversation circle says.[33]

Of course, the flip side of this reciprocity coin is not only that I will listen to and take seriously what you have to say, but also that when I "proclaim" what I have experienced, what I have thought to be true and meaningful, I do so in a manner that is *tentative.* In other words, I express myself to engage and advance the conversation, not to shut it down. I am not apologetic for my thoughts and beliefs, but even as I speak I am aware of the limitations of my insight and of my constant need for conversion. I express my opinion with the desire of having it tested by the community for the sake of my and everyone else's conversion. Indeed, for conversations to advance and conversions to be possible, the ethic of reciprocity must include both an egalitarian view of our conversation partners and a valuing of difference among our proclamation partners. If everyone around the table agrees, if everyone shares the same experiences and knowledge, there is little about which to converse.[34] Instead of being mutually converted, we will simply be mutually confirmed in our limited understanding of God, self, and the world. This could hardly be called proclamation. When I speak in the midst of the church's conversations, I should not be looking to have the last word. Rather, my words should be a response to words that have gone before and lead into words that will follow. I hope that my proclamation invites both complementary and contradictory proclamation from others. Only thus will I be challenged to grow in my faith and in my meaning-making process and will I be able to challenge others to grow in theirs.

Content of the Conversation

Next we need to consider what topics are appropriate for the church's conversations. This is no small question.[35] However, for the purposes of this book, the answer need not be long.

The church has too often taken an isolationist approach to what it discusses. One need not spend much time reviewing sermons, Christian education literature, and church newsletters to see how narrow and "churchy" our church talk has been. But as we have noted, we live in a time that is saturated with a cacophony of "talk." People consciously and unconsciously make meaning in conversation with everyone and everything they read, hear, and see. If the church engages only in insider conversation, we can expect to influence only a small portion of what people count as meaningful in their lives and in the world. Therefore, church talk must embrace a much wider range of topics, issues, and experiences than it does now.

Beyond the practical reason of influence for expanding the content of the church's proclamatory conversations is a theological one—the historic claim that God is *omnipresent*. By professing God as being eternally everywhere (whether we are constantly aware of the divine presence or not), the church asserts that there is no realm of human experience or inquiry that is unrelated to ultimate meaning. This move to ground the church's proclamation in divine omnipresence has affinities with Mary Catherine Hilkert's proposal to expand Protestant theologies of preaching that "have been constructed in terms of a biblical theology of the word or in terms that highlight the transcendence of God's word" with "a Catholic perspective that views grace as active in and through humanity and describes revelation in sacramental terms."[36] Hilkert follows Rahner, Schillebeeckx, and liberation theology in affirming the sacramental imagination that views divine grace as "here . . . present wherever we are."[37] At the core of Christian proclamation for Hilkert, therefore, is naming the divine grace that is part and parcel of the giftedness of human existence.

This sort of universal theological claim concerning divine omnipresence has the ring of a metanarrative, and, of course, this is problematic since metanarratives are rejected by postmodern culture. But a few observations will clarify my proposal. As I have already noted, while the authority of metanarratives to define the worldviews *of all* is rejected in cultural postmodernism, individual and group efforts at creating cohesive worldviews is not. In other words, we may not force our views on others and need not accept their views as ours, but we adopt, adapt, and construct metanarratives that inform and interpret our particular existence. Moreover, even though my concern is to develop a proposal for authentic Christian proclamation in a postmodern culture, it is important to remember that Christianity is not at root a postmodern phenomenon but an ancient and ongoing and evolving metanarrative. One way (among many possible approaches) of *using* the Christian metanarrative in a postmodern fashion, however, is to ground the church's conversational proclamation in individual experiences of divine omnipresence. Paul Scherer's words ring true differently in this postmodern context than in the mid-twentieth century in which he first expressed them: "The only final authority in life is the defenseless authority of an eternal presence."[38]

Indeed, in terms of congregations' proclamatory conversations, the claim that God is present in every experience translates into the dictum that *no topic should be considered off-limits* in the church's conversations because God is in it all. It should be safe to raise any issue or question in the church's conversation, as long as the person doing so is sincere and respectful. Topics are limited only by the shared interests, experiences, and identities of the conversation partners as they strive to make meaning of God, self, and the world, not by some preconceived notion of theological, pious, or moral appropriateness.

This does not mean, however, that any approach to a topic is appropriate for the church's proclamatory conversations. At root, what makes a conversation appropriate for the church is less the topic and more the language used to address and examine it. Ecclesial conversations, even postmodern ecclesial conversations, should presume *Christian language*. In the church we can converse about politics, war, sex, theodicy, the economy, art, health issues, Taoism, race issues, psychology, the church building, ecology, gender issues, the Trinity, movies, addiction, evolution, computer technology, parenting, the book of Revelation, music, and domestic violence, but if the conversation is to be proclamatory, it must use and be shaped by the language of the Christian faith. In other words, we do not limit our talk to "Christian" topics, but we do covenant to bring Christian traditions to bear on any topic we discuss as we individually and communally make meaning in relation to these different topics. Only then can the conversations lead to the kinds of mutual conversion the church as the body of Christ should value. Only then can the conversation be called Christian proclamation.[39]

Conversational Etiquette

Different types of conversation in the church require different structures and different rules of etiquette. A personal comment that is appropriate in one conversation circle may not be in another. A strong ideological stance may be offensive in one circle and readily heard in another. Some conversations will be strictly structured around a narrow topic or agenda while others may flow with no restrictions. Some conversations will be one-time occasions, and others may stretch over months or years. Some conversations will be topic oriented, and others formed primarily to create fellowship and support. These sorts of differences mean that it is possible to make only general observations about processes that are appropriate for the wide range of proclamatory conversations in the church.

Burbules offers three rules or principles of dialogue that inform an etiquette of pedagogical conversation.[40] They are also good guides for ecclesial conversations. We have already discussed one above—the rule of *reciprocity*, an egalitarian interest, respect, and concern that conversation partners share for one another and for the give-and-take conversational process as they go about the task of proclaiming their experience and interpretation of the presence of God.

The second is the rule of *participation*. If a conversation is to be truly reciprocal, and thus invite mutual conversion, all participants must be *active* participants. Everyone must be able and willing to offer opinions, pose questions, challenge differing points of view, and be challenged by different points of view.[41] As Michael F. Schober notes, every utterance in a conversation is merely an attempt to be understood without any guarantee that understanding will actually be achieved. He writes, "The general flavor . . . is that what is meant is subject to negotiation, that the conversation partner helps shape the speaker's utterances, and that what a speaker says isn't necessarily adequate and may need fixing."[42] Therefore, the active participation of everyone gathered around the circle is absolutely necessary. At the same time, no one should be allowed to act in a manner that prohibits the full participation of others, be it in the form of diminishing someone's views or by monopolizing the floor.[43] Structures need to be in place to allow for and encourage the full, active participation of all partners if the conversation is to have any of the liberating power of the gospel.[44]

Burbules's third general principle for dialogue is the rule of *commitment*. As he writes, "Consensus may be too much to hope for. . . . But some degree of understanding of one another's views, and the thoughts, feelings, and experiences that underlie them, is usually *not* too much to hope for."[45] For such understanding to arise and become edifying in the church, participants must be committed to the conversation and to their conversation partners even when difficult and divisive concerns are raised. We have already discussed the kind of commitment to one's conversation partners that is required by an ethic of trust and reciprocity, but what does it mean to be committed to the conversation itself? It means that we trust that conversations in the body of Christ will lead, in some way or another, to God-in-Christ. It means that we must not only be willing to offer our sincere proclamation of our experience and understanding of God, self, and the world in relation to whatever particular topic we are discussing and but also be open to challenges and questions concerning our views and the underlying reasons, feelings, and motivations for holding them.

The Goal

While a clear agenda or narrow topic may be the reason for gathering a group to engage in conversation, in any situation that truly embraces give-

and-take interaction, freedom must exist for the conversation to evolve.[46] This does not mean that the rule for ecclesial conversation is "Anything goes." Depending on the focus that has gathered in the conversation circle, on the one hand, and the ethos and will of the community, on the other, limits can and should be placed on appropriate directions for the conversation to evolve. Nevertheless, a certain *openendedness* must be part of the very definition of the church's conversations, a flow to the conversation that can be appropriately limited, disciplined, even directed, but not controlled. Each contribution is unique and has a unique impact on the conversation itself and resulting comments. Beginnings of conversations may be strictly defined, but never endings.

In choosing the term "conversation" to designate the kind of proclamatory discourse we are promoting, I have already claimed that the goal of the church's conversations is *conversion*. In light of the openendedness I have just claimed for conversations, it needs to be said that this conversion must not be predetermined in any except the most general ways. We can say that we want all conversation participants to be converted in the sense of growing in their understanding, relationship to, and interaction with God, self, and the world in light of Christ traditions, and that we want the conversational community to be transformed by both the tensions and the mutual understandings that occur in the process of conversing. But we must resist the temptation to determine in advance (and thus manipulate) how such growth should manifest itself in the participants, including ourselves, or in the congregation as a whole. Indeed, the conversion that occurs may not, and probably should not, be the same for every individual involved; and such unrestricted diversity of transformation will determine the nature of communal conversion. We should seek neither forced intellectual consensus nor *koinonia* that is in reality forced conformity. The wind blows where it will, and to try futilely to control it is to stifle the manifestation of the Spirit in conversational proclamation.

The Conversational Dilemma

The question that now rises is how to engage postmodern congregations in this kind of conversation. We should not be so naïve as to imagine that it will be a simple task. In the first place, much of the church's discourse has been dominated by monologue (preaching) and debate (whether theological or administrative). To create a community in which no authority figure has the last word and in which no one wins or loses an argument requires a reversal of these tendencies.

In the second place, while changing our view of proclamation from a monological declaration of universal truth to a give-and-take approach that gives participants the freedom to make meaning out of what is said fits with a postmodern epistemology, the level of individual commitment and participation required in the kind of ecclesial conversations we have described goes against current cultural tendencies toward isolation and individualism. This situation is well described by John L. Locke, who writes, "In our modern, complex societies we are suffering from a social form of progressive aphonia. That is, we are losing our personal voices. During a period in which feelings of isolation and loneliness are on the rise, too many of us are becoming emotionally and socially mute."[47] He identifies historical developments and current factors that have converged to cause this phenomenon.

- *Urbanization*—We have shifted from a culture of small intimate communities in which the self is affirmed to urban centers of masses of strangers.
- *Literacy*—As more of Western society has become literate, information can be exchanged in one direction to great masses without requiring any face-to-face exchange.
- *Atomization*—One of the legacies of the Enlightenment that has increased in postmodernism is the rise of the individual. Communities no longer share unilateral values, and their shared experiences are surface experiences of watching the same television programs, eating at the same restaurant chains, and living in the same region.
- *Solo sapiens*—The rise of the individual has led Americans to value social insulation. Our front porches have been replaced by backyard decks surrounded by privacy fences. The number of people participating in civic, social, religious, and recreational communities is decreasing.[48]
- *Relocation*—The phenomenon of relocation that began with migration to urban centers is to a great extent now reversed with people migrating to suburbs. Such moves imply leaving behind one's social structures and relationships to live near but not necessarily know other people with similar histories.
- *Need to Know*—The combination of monadic living, the rapid pace of change in contemporary society, and high-speed communication systems has resulted in a culture of individuals being fed and tasting a constant stream of information. Little of the information, however, gets digested, much less discussed, in any significant way in community.

- *Loss of the Great Good Place*—Both a cause and a result of the de-voicing of America is the loss of places where people gather to talk in causal community. Local stores have been replaced by large chain superstores, and the water cooler at work has been replaced with e-mail.
- *Totally Tubular*—Television has made a people of passive reception, with 98 percent of American homes having at least one TV set. The homes are filled with talk, but not of those living there. Studies show that the amount of talk in homes has decreased significantly with the rise of addiction to televised entertainment.
- *Too Busy to Talk*—As technology, information, and mobility have increased, American life has become busier. We live with a "What's next?" attitude in America. The forty-hour work week is rarely the norm any longer. Commuting from home to work adds to this. And then time saved by household conveniences is given to the television.
- *Decline of Trust*—All of the factors of de-voicing mentioned thus far spiral into a decline of trust in which we do not talk to one another out of suspicion of the stranger (xenophobia). Estrangement begets distrust and indeed lack of trustworthiness. The fewer people we know as Subjects, the less we respect their ability to have our best interests at heart and the less we are concerned with their best interests.

The church will not have an easy time overcoming such obstacles and creating itself as a community of theological conversation, becoming a great, good place in which the body of Christ gathers to proclaim the gospel in give-and-take fashion. But it is not impossible. To become such a community will require the patience to move slowly[49] and intentional efforts to inventory, nurture, change, and expand the church's conversations. It is not in the scope of this book nor is it in my expertise to prescribe detailed methods for shaping a congregation into such a community of conversation. However, it is unfair (in preaching or in writing a book about preaching) to propose an ought without any hint of prescribing a how, and the partial ecclesiology I have offered calls me to offer some broad, practical suggestions.

Although much of congregational speech is dominated by monologue and debate, and although our culture has diminished the importance once placed on the interpersonal and communal development that grew out of conversation, there have always been and still are small pockets of conversation in the church that reflect or come close to the kind of conversation we have described and prescribed above. Thus any pastor or congregation wishing to develop more fully a community of conversational proclamation must begin with an *inventory* of current church talk. Where is church talk monological? Argumentative? Conversational? Which conversation circles are hierarchical and which are egalitarian? This inventory will allow the congregation to identify the best forms of conversation within the congregation to use as a foundation for developing an authentically conversational community of faith.

Next the pastor, church staff, and congregation should *nurture* the conversation circles that best embrace the ethics and etiquette of conversation described above. These internal examples of authentic conversation and not some external model should be the foundation for a congregational homiletic. This means that a significant part of the process of nurture, especially early on, will include explicit, *conversational reflection* on the process of conversation itself as manifested in these circles and in the church as a whole.[50]

In a manner that is appropriate for the individual congregation, these conversation circles and the reflection process on the kind of conversation they share should slowly and gently be used to *influence* other arenas of church talk. Where can hierarchy be replaced with a reciprocity that still values leadership? Where can unnecessary debate be changed into conversation and where can necessary debate be influenced by a conversational attitude? Where can unnecessary monologue be replaced with conversation and necessary monologue be influenced by a conversational approach to the community and to proclamation? In other words, how can all of our church talk be sanctified in the sense that it becomes part of the sacred conversation of the body of Christ proclaiming the gospel in give-and-take fashion?

In the midst of this process of nurture and change, there should also be, slowly and as appropriate, an *expansion* of opportunities for conversation in the church. By increasing the number of conversation circles to represent a wider diversity of conversational topics, degrees of commitment, structures, and times, more members of the body of Christ will find a place (or a number of places) where they feel comfortable proclaiming their experience and knowledge of God and learning from others.[51]

All of these steps will incorporate the slow process of *trust building*. Trust that the conversations are valuable. Trust that conversation partners will be supportive and reciprocal. But, while it can be frustrating, a slow pace is appropriate to the nature of conversation itself. The conversions that take place in conversation are more often minute transformations than radical U-turns. Likewise, as individual conversations in the church slowly evolve, the church as a community of conversation will also slowly evolve. As individuals are converted bit by bit, so will the community comprising those individuals be changed.

The Matrix of Conversations

All of these nurtured, changed, and new conversation circles can overlap and connect into a *matrix of conversations* that over time will transform the postmodern church into a vital community of give-and-take proclamation that is appropriate to the age in which we find ourselves. Indeed, such a matrix of conversations will not only empower individuals to engage and struggle with the Christian traditions in their own meaning-making process but will shape the way the community (as a group of believers in but not of the world) understands its broad institutional mission as the body of Christ, struggling to transform the world instead of being conformed to it. It is essential therefore that great attention be given to the way the matrix of conversations is shaped—that there be diversity and balance in the range of opportunities a church offers to its people and to the world to encounter and proclaim the gospel.

It is helpful, therefore, to develop a *taxonomy of conversations* in the church, so that we can properly inventory, nurture, change, and expand these opportunities as we go about the task of reenlivening the church's proclamation. If the character of the church's proclamation is determined in the first place by the character of the church as a *gathering*, then one way to create such a catalog of conversations is simply to evaluate why different conversation circles are gathered. In what follows I designate four broad types of conversational gatherings. This list is meant to be neither exhaustive nor precise. Many other examples of conversation circles could be listed, and some of the examples I offer could easily be placed in more than one category. The goal of offering this taxonomy is simply to get some tools on the table that we can use in evaluating where a church's conversational strengths and weaknesses are.

1. Some conversation circles gather together people based on *shared characteristics of identity*. These include groups gathered on the basis of age (children, youth, adult, older adult); gender (men and women); life situations (singles, singles again, parents, support/encounter groups); broad concerns (social justice, spirituality); and so on and so forth. These conversation circles are usually longstanding groups or at least longstanding structures. Christian education structures in congregations are usually

dominated by these gatherings. Topics of conversation are less determinative for the groups than are the shared identities; in fact, topics can change often while the group remains the same. What makes these groups different from shared identity groups outside the church is that one element of their shared identity is that they are part of the body of Christ. As such, the conversation partners agree that whatever they discuss will be brought into contact with Christian traditions. For example, singles groups do not simply gather in the church to meet and greet but also to bring Christian perspectives to bear on their lives as singles and to bring their perspectives as singles to bear on Christian traditions.

2. The second type of conversational gathering is *issue- or topic-oriented conversations*, in which the community is secondary to the topic. Such conversational circles are usually only together for a short term compared with the shared-identity circles. Once the issue has been discussed thoroughly, the conversation circle may disband. As mentioned earlier, churches need to expand their conversational repertoire beyond church topics if we are to hope that Christian traditions will have any impact on the people's attempts at making meaning in the much broader matrix of conversations that make up their lives. Opportunities for such conversations should of course include traditional church issues like Bible study, doctrine, and denominational history and beliefs, but also political, economic, sociological, interfaith, literary, historical, and philosophical conversations. In sum, no topic or issue should be considered inappropriate if there are members of the congregation interested in the topic. Again, however, for the conversations to be Christian proclamation, the topics must be considered from Christian perspectives, must use Christian language, and must engage Christian traditions in relation to the topic.

3. The third type of conversational gathering in the church is that of *administrative conversations*. In practice, business meetings in the church rarely have the quality of authentic conversation I am promoting, but they should. Although decisions have to be made and there may be at times winners and losers, church debates can be made healthier and indeed even proclamatory if they are influenced by the conversational virtues I have described and by the broader matrix of conversations throughout the church. Moreover, if partners in administrative conversations see themselves as proclaiming the gospel to one another even in that setting, surely the tone of many such meetings will change.

4. The final category of conversational gatherings is *worship*. Worship must certainly be considered the prime reason the church gathers, but we rarely think of this type of gathering as conversational. As administrative

conversations have been dominated by argument, worship has been dominated by monologue. Whether we are talking about preaching, prayer, or music, most worship involves a few leaders presenting something for the rest to receive. Indeed, even in most African American and Pentecostal congregations where those in the pews are speaking out, *true* conversation is still absent. If worship is truly to be liturgy (i.e., the work of the people), then this must change. This does not mean, however, that preachers must engage in dialogue sermons or that the worshiping congregation must be divided into breakout groups. For most churches, worship will always and should always have the character of a mixture of shared work (congregational singing, unison prayers, offering, etc.) and presentation (anthems, pastoral prayer, sermons).

Worship can, however, be transformed from a hierarchical, absolute-truth-oriented model, in which the worship leaders (the preacher in particular) pour out the gospel in order to fill the congregation, to a model in which the worship service and the sermon in particular make a contribution to the matrix of conversations going on throughout the church. What is offered in worship is influenced by what is being proclaimed throughout the church and in turn strives to make a contribution to what is being proclaimed throughout the church. In other words, the worship service is a part of, instead of apart from, the give-and-take matrix of conversation that is the church's proclamation. It is to this contribution that I turn in the next chapter.

Chapter 3

A Conversational Homiletic

In ordinary conversation one usually feels oppressed by those who force an argument or a position upon one on their terms, allowing space only to agree or disagree. One feels liberated by those who offer new ideas for reflection or open new angles of vision on familiar things. The word *preaching* has come to have negative connotations because so much of it, following many theories of preaching, has the former character.

—William Beardslee, et al.[1]

In chapter 1, we reviewed earlier suggestions for integrating conversation and preaching. Each of the three models—conversation during the sermon, conversation before the sermon, and conversational sermons—offers much to those struggling to proclaim the gospel authentically in a postmodern era, but are not, in themselves, satisfactory solutions. I have attempted to build on these proposals by arguing that the sermon should not be the focus of the conversation but a part of the matrix of ongoing conversations that encompasses the entire life and mission of the congregation.

Therefore, in chapter 2 I developed an abbreviated ecclesiology of the church as a community of theological conversation, meaning by "theological," all discussion related to making meaning of God, self, and the world. In this postmodern understanding of the church, proclamation is not the sole responsibility or possession of the preacher. Indeed, the good news is proclaimed in a give-and-take fashion; everyone proclaims his or her knowledge, experience, and interpretation of God-in-Christ, and everyone listens as others proclaim. The result of this form of conversational proclamation is mutual turning, or con-version. This prescription for the church involved not just theological conceptualization but also broad, practical implications concerning the appropriate manner in which conversation should be conducted in the gathering that is the body of Christ.

This discussion has prepared us to narrow our focus now from a homiletical ecclesiology to an ecclesiological homiletic. In this chapter I propose a conversational theology of preaching, and in the next I explore its practical implications. In other words, we turn now to the role of the preacher in the matrix of proclamatory conversations that are central in the meaning-making process of postmodern individuals and in the life of the postmodern congregation as a whole. *How does the monological sermon function in a conversational approach to proclamation?*

The question facing us is at the root of every theology of preaching: What is the purpose of preaching and how does that purpose determine how one preaches? It should be obvious from the conversational view of proclamation I propose that the purpose of preaching is not to be defined hierarchically in terms of the preacher pouring out the good news from above to the people below in the way that many claims of the preacher's authority and purpose have traditionally been configured. Instead, in our ecclesiological, conversational homiletic, the preacher is one of many conversation partners in the church.

Of course, there is no denying, nor is there any reason to deny, that the pastor who preaches each week has a privileged voice, for worship is the one regular time in which the church invites a monologue into its theological conversation. In what follows, therefore, I explore the nature of this privilege, that is, the nature of the authority of the pulpit in the context of the matrix of proclamatory conversations. At this early point, it may be prudent to recall that much of our understanding of ecclesiological conversation was adapted from pedagogical approaches that use conversation in the classroom. My interest in these approaches arose, to a great degree, because the struggle to understand the preacher's authority in a congregation in which proclamation happens in the mode of conversation is analogous to teachers having to address the issue of their privilege and authority in an egalitarian approach to the classroom as a conversational community. Nicholas C. Burbules, whom we have drawn on a great deal, acknowledges that some scholars have questioned whether *any* conception of a teacher having legitimate authority is compatible with the spirit of egalitarian learning, but he also reminds us that asymmetry is necessary for good conversation:

I do not see how we can avoid some sort of authority in every educational endeavor, no matter how earnestly we strive for egalitarian communicative relations; nor is authority necessarily a threat to egalitarian relations. We often seek out information from a better-informed source, advice from an experienced mentor, insight from a friend who knows us well, direction from a group facilitator, and so on. These are all instances of authority. While it is essential that credible authority not be taken for granted but be periodically scrutinized and re-established, this scrutiny cannot take place continuously, and at particular moments such authority will be an unstated element in an ongoing dialogical relation. The question ought to be framed: What *types* of educational authority are justified?[2]

Similarly, as part of this study of the role of the monological sermon in a conversational community, we must ask what types of proclamatory authority can justifiably be asserted on behalf of the preacher.

Of course, any assertions concerning the authority of the preacher must begin with the claim that, while standing in the pulpit, the preacher fully *participates* in the community's give-and-take proclamation of the gospel. The question concerning the purpose of preaching that lies before us, then, is really the issue of how preaching, as a regularly (i.e., weekly) privileged voice, appropriately participates in the matrix of conversations that echoes throughout the body of Christ. We should immediately dismiss any idea that preaching is the beginning, center, or end of the conversation. Indeed, the sermon is neither the origin of the church's conversation, the focus of it, nor the final word in it. The preacher is one voice among many in a conversation that precedes and outlasts her. She is one conversation partner among many partners who are proclaiming the gospel and listening to others proclaim the gospel. But, as we shall see, this shift in the theology of preaching that I am proposing does not marginalize or devalue the pulpit. Instead, it places the pulpit in its proper place—actively participating in the congregation's conversation circles by offering a specialized voice in the give-and-take proclamation of the church. While the congregation's proclamatory conversations could go on without preaching, a great gift to the conversation would be lost if the pulpit were left empty.

Preaching out of Reciprocity

For the preaching office of the church to participate in the matrix of ongoing, proclamatory conversations in the body of Christ, instead of standing above it or at its center, the preacher must adhere to the church's conversational ethics and etiquette even when he is speaking in a single voice from the pulpit. The preacher must be trusting and trustworthy, sincere and honest; value both common points of view and asymmetry; and be committed to the conversation beyond moments of either consensus or utter tension. But, of course, at the center of the church's roundtable is a small stone tablet reminding all who would gather to converse and be converted of the most important conversational principle: the covenant of egalitarian reciprocity. For the preacher this principle of reciprocity means that if she wishes to be heard, she listen as others proclaim their experience and interpretation of God, self, and the world, just like everyone else who participates in the sacred conversation of meaning making in the church. The foundation on which the pulpit rests is the give-and-take relationship that exists among/throughout the congregation. As moments of debate in the church should be shaped by conversation, so should moments of monologue, especially sermons. Before stepping into the pulpit, the preacher must be fully immersed in the matrix of conversations that is central to the mission of the community of faith and to the meaning-making process of its individual members. This means he must be on both sides of the give-and-take nature of proclamation, not just the giving side. In other words, if preachers want to have something to say to today's congregations and want to be taken seriously by them, they must first close their mouths and cup their ears.[3]

But we must be clear. The listening that is called for is not that of a passive, distant, unaffected observer, who overhears a conversation in order to cull materials to use as illustrations in a sermon. Nor is this an over-and-above listening like that of a school teacher who listens as students struggle with knowledge that the teacher could easily dispense but who withholds for the sake of the learning process of the children. Rather, the preacher practices *reciprocal listening*; it is risky, open-minded, willing-and-wanting-to-be-converted listening. The preacher actively participates in the conversations not only as (nor even primarily as) a professional clergyperson charged with the vocational task of leading a congregation in its ministries but as a Christian struggling to make meaning of God, self, and the world with the "language" of the Christian faith as her primary (but not only) meaning-making resource. Preaching, in other words, is *in no way* set apart from the matrix of conversations that comprise the church but instead participates in the conversation completely. This is similar to what Paulo Friere argues must happen for education to be liberating: "Through dialogue, the teacher-of-the-students and the students-of-the-teacher cease to exist and a new term emerges: teacher-student and student-teachers. . . . They become jointly responsible for a process in which all grow."[4] The preacher must be committed to the congregation's conversations and claim all contributions to those conversations as proclamation that is as important to the church's witness as his own preaching, albeit different in character. Indeed, he must existentially embrace other voices in the congregation as proclamation offered to him.

Preaching Reformed and Always to Be Reformed

Viewing the preacher as fully participating in the receiving end of the give-and-take of the church's conversations implies a serious revision of the modern church's inheritance of the reformers' claim that the sermon event is to be equated with the Word of God.[5] For our purposes, we need not distinguish between Luther's and Calvin's nuanced developments of this theme. In general, for the Reformers, God speaks the Word through Christ, through Scripture, and through preaching. T. H. L. Parker summarizes the Reformation view of preaching in this manner:

> The reason for the great weight that the Reformers laid on preaching was not educational or social but theological. . . . The real reason is to be found in the Biblical concept of the Word of God. 'The Word of God' so easily becomes a catch-phrase of weak and uncertain meaning that we have to remind ourselves that for the Reformers it had enormous significance, fresh, living, explosive. 'The Word of God' meant 'the Word that God himself speaks'. It was the Word of God that created the universe; that is, God spoke and what he said called into being that which had not been. It was by his Word that God in his free majesty encountered man. 'The Word' was a synonym for the Son of God who became man and who lived among men as the living declaration of God's eternal will to man. 'The Word' was also the creative utterance of the Word made flesh; his words brought Lazarus again from the dead; his words give life to the world; his words are cleansing; his words will judge men at the last day. But then, as the Reformers read the Acts of the Apostles and the Epistles, they perceived that the preaching of the apostles and evangelists was also called 'the Word of God' or 'the Word of the Lord'. So that it was necessary to regard the terms 'Gospel', 'preaching', and 'Word of God' as synonymous.[6]

As the Second Helvetic Confession puts it, "Preaching the Word of God *is* the Word of God" (italics added). Or in Luther's words, "the preacher's mouth and the words that I hear are not his; they are the words and message of the Holy Spirit [through which] He works within me and thus He makes me holy."[7] If, through the Holy Spirit, the preacher's words are or become God's Word (in some unique, sacramental sense that distinguishes it from other forms of speech[8]), then sermons, although they may do other things, are above all encounters with God.[9] The Reformers inherited from the medieval church a theology of the sacraments that involved the real presence of God, and to this they added a new understanding of preaching as offering the real presence of God to those gathered to listen. This transformed worship from a seeing liturgy (in terms of the congregation watching the sacraments administered for them in Latin) into a hearing liturgy (in terms of the congregation listening to the Word proclaimed to them in their vernacular), but those gathered to worship remained in a largely passive role while the clergy actively served as the vessel of God's presence.[10]

Although it can be variously nuanced, especially in terms of viewing the hearers as active instead of passive recipients of the sermon, this understanding of preaching as a unique Word event has prevailed in twentieth-century preaching and homiletics. And, indeed, the evolution of this understanding of the sermon has served the church well in modernity. However, this Word-of-God homiletical theology has less to offer the postmodern approach to making meaning than it did to an Enlightenment approach to discovering truth. A preacher who begins the task of preaching by listening to the proclamation of others offered in give-and-take fashion in a setting where people are suspicious of authoritarian claims of holding and pronouncing truth cannot be comfortable with this traditional hegemony of God's Word and God's presence claimed for preaching. The purpose of the pulpit must not be defined in terms of a *special* event that mysteriously conveys God's presence.[11] Instead, it must be related to the omnipresence of God that is proclaimed *throughout* the church's conversation. Indeed, it is this conversation as a whole (including but not limited to preaching) that resonates with, even though it is not equivalent to, the Word of God. As Mary Catherine Hilkert comments,

> Precisely because of the conviction that God's word is spoken also in the experience of people's lives, liberation theologians remark that preaching is most effective when members of the community are

encouraged to tell their own stories. The focus is on the word of God heard in community reflection on daily life and political struggles in light of the scriptures, rather than on the proclamation of an individual preacher or priest.[12]

Photographic Homiletic

The claim that God is everywhere implies three things about the congregation's give-and-take proclamation. First, if God is everywhere, then *everyone* has experienced God and can participate in give-and-take God-talk. They can proclaim what they experience, think, feel, believe, and interpret to be meaningful at an ultimate level. And what they experience, think, feel, believe, and interpret to be meaningful will evolve as they listen to and reflect on the experiences, thoughts, emotions, faith, and interpretations of others. Second, by professing God as being eternally everywhere, the church asserts that there is no realm of human experience or knowledge that is unrelated to claims of ultimate meaning. In terms of congregations' conversational proclamation, this claim means that no topic should be considered off-limits in the church's conversations because God is in it all.

Third, and specifically related to the pulpit, by anchoring this conversational approach to proclamation in the doctrine of divine omnipresence instead of the doctrine of the Word of God, we no longer view the sermon as a unique event in which God's presence is conveyed to those gathered. Instead of primarily providing or conveying God's presence, the preacher's task is to *point* to the divine presence that is constantly a part of everything experienced by the individuals gathered and by the congregation as a whole.

This is no easy task, for the scientific age has led us far away from our ancestors' sense of the sacredness of the universe and daily events. Even though we may claim God is everywhere, we experience God as playing hide-and-seek with us. God is no longer evident in the blessings of rain or the misfortunes of drought; the Weather Channel explains differences in rainfall in terms of natural fronts and cycles. We no longer think of God as sitting in heaven above constantly watching us; after all, our telescopes, rockets, and satellites have actually explored the heavens. Although many are certainly thankful to God for the blessing of children, those who have trouble having children turn quickly from prayer to fertility specialists. The list of distinctions between prescientific worldviews (dominated by theistic explanations of the world) and scientific worldviews (dominated by materialist explanations of the world) could go on and on. But suffice it to say that, for the most part, both modern and postmodern people are simply no longer attuned to a sense of the divine as constantly present in the commonplace, otherwise explainable aspects of life and of the world.

The tasks of the postmodern preacher, therefore, are to help congregations *re-member*—in other words to recall and to piece together again—the presence of God in their lives, participate in the struggle to name *how* God is present in any given moment, and determine the significance of the experienced divine presence to their understanding of God, self, and the world. To claim that God (who is paradoxically both mercy and justice) is utterly present in personal, communal, and international relationships; in making love and in the horrors of oppression; and in moments of birth and of death is to call for a different way of viewing the quality and potential of every moment of existence and how we are to act in those moments. In other words, the preacher who points to God's omnipresence is inviting those who have gathered to worship to make meaning, indeed to make ultimate meaning, of their lives and their world.

To speak metaphorically, preachers act like *photographers*, taking pictures of the world and the congregation's experiences and offering them to the congregation for their consideration.[13] Through their homiletical cameras, they artistically offer new perspectives of what the congregation has been looking at all along. It is important to recognize that the task of congregational proclamation, as I have described it, is really no different from what any other person gathered at the conversational roundtable is invited and able to do. Nor should it be. All are invited to the conversational table to witness to God's presence and to offer an interpretation of that presence.

There is a difference, however, between the contribution made to the conversation from the pulpit and the contribution of others, and it lies in the training and equipment preachers bring with them to the task of offering proclamatory snapshots of God's presence in the world. This training and the continued use of the perspectives and skills developed as a consequence of that training is the basis of the privilege and authority the congregation offers to the preacher. Through seminary education, ordination, the pastoral office of serving a specific congregation, and a life of study in which the preacher, on behalf of the congregation, continually struggles to link Christian traditions with the whole of existence, the preacher brings a professional, trained eye to the photographer's task. Preachers see differently: What others see as coincidence, they see as providence. What others see as tragic, they see as sinful. What others see as change, they see as resurrection. What others see as scandal, they see as redemptive. In sum, when others see the ordinary, the preacher sees God. Through earlier

That's offensive

courses and continued reflection on systematic theology, ethics, biblical studies, pastoral theology, church history, religion and the arts, hermeneutics, liturgy, and homiletics, the preacher continues to develop a specialized "trained eye" on behalf of the congregation that gathers to offer proclamation in conversation with each other and with the world.

This "continued reflection" needs to be strongly emphasized for a conversational homiletic, or for any homiletic. Good preaching takes a lot of time and requires the preacher to be a thoughtful, studied person. If the unique contribution pastors bring to the congregation's meaning-making conversation is rooted in their having been set apart by the church to study the church's witness to God's presence in the world, then continued, constant study needs to be a priority on the pastor's job description. Congregations consistently claim that the primary thing they want out of their pastor is a good preacher, and pastors consistently bemoan the fact that the long list of other administrative and pastoral duties take away the time they need to prepare better sermons. So congregations need to reclaim the significance of having a pastor's *study*, instead of a pastor's office. And they need not simply tolerate time that their pastor spends in solitude in that space, but demand that she or he spend more time in there on their behalf and celebrate when he or she is able to do so.

Composition

A preacher with such a trained eye has a great deal of freedom concerning what subject to photograph for an individual sermon as it contributes to the ongoing proclamatory conversation of the church. Everything in her field of vision is fair game, for the Holy Spirit is alive and well in it all. But how is the preacher to choose a subject to photograph? By what criteria does she, using her training, compose or frame it? As real estate value is determined, so the saying goes, by location, location, location, so in homiletical photography the appropriateness of a particular contribution to the proclamatory conversation is determined by context, context, context. In fact, I would suggest that the preacher should consider six homiletical contexts when deciding how to compose a photograph of God's presence and its implications on any given Sunday: the personal, congregational, theological, sociohistorical, liturgical, and conversational.[14] These contexts rarely change radically from week to week. They evolve subtly over time, however. Thus, while it may not be important to spend much energy examining these contexts each week, it is helpful if the preacher performs regular contextual inventories.

what are preachers bringing

1. The *personal context*. Preaching is an incarnational act. Like everyone else in the matrix of conversation circles in the church, preachers are subjective beings whose vision is shaped by their histories, presuppositions, values, theologies, personal experiences, ideologies, memories, and doubts. What preachers offer to the matrix of proclamatory conversations from the pulpit is intimately related to their psychological, physical, social, intellectual, and spiritual state. The more self-aware a preacher is, the better the preaching will be. As she decides what snapshot to offer in a sermon, she must take her own pulse, asking, What issues engage me right now? How is my physical and mental health? What is going on in my life, in my family, in my ministry? What is the current tone of my relationship with the congregation?

who are the hearers

2. The *congregational context*. Having a good grasp of the ethos of the particular community to which one is preaching is essential for effective preaching. Without having a sense of what is on the minds and in the hearts of those sitting in the pews, the preacher will offer a sermon that passes by them like a rock skipping over water. As he chooses what photograph to present to the congregation, the preacher must take their pulse in the same fashion that he takes his own, asking himself, What is the history of the congregation and what do I hope its future will be? What is the makeup of the congregation in terms of socioeconomic status, race, gender, age, and educational level? Is there unity or tension in the congregation? Are we a gathering of individual strangers or a close-knit community? What arenas of ministry and mission are/should we be involved in?[15]

3. The *theological context*. As the preacher conceives sermon topics, themes, or ideas, she should reflect on their connection to systematic theology and the history of doctrine. The particular sermonic focus she offers to the congregation's conversation will be better received by the hearers if she has a firm grasp on and is able to convey the relationship between that focus and a comprehensive Christian theological outlook.[16] A particularly helpful question for the preacher to ask is, What are the connections of this potential sermonic focus to this particular denominational tradition's theology and this particular congregation's theological leanings?

4. The *sociohistorical context*. God's presence is not found in the church alone, but in the whole of creation. If the preacher expects his sermon to have an impact on the hearers' lives outside their participation in the congregation, he must consider the world beyond the walls and history of the church in shaping his sermons and ask, What is going on in the community, state, country, and world that shapes the way we should approach any conversation topic related to ultimate concern? How does what is going

on "out there" affect the church and the individual Christian? Conversely, how is/should the church and its individual members be affecting what is going on "out there"?

These four contexts—the personal, congregational, theological, and sociohistorical—can be viewed as four overlapping circles in a Vin Diagram.

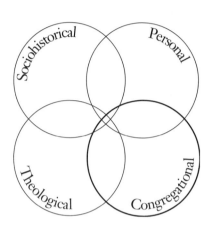

Such an arrangement illustrates the manner in which these contexts are equally important for the preacher to consider and are intimately related to each other but not coterminous. Preachers should strive to compose each particular homiletical snapshot that demonstrates, in some way, God's presence at the intersection of these contexts for that particular occasion.

The next two contexts, however, are not simply equal, overlapping contexts. These are central to choosing the homiletical photograph.

5. The *liturgical context*. The particular worship service for which a sermon is being developed is of central concern for the preacher because the liturgy as a whole should engage the personal, congregational, theological, and sociohistorical contexts. The sermon should join together with music, prayers, and sacraments to relate the gospel to these contexts. Too often, however, worship is planned like a pot-luck dinner where the salads, meats, side dishes, and desserts are not coordinated. It is important that, as the preacher composes her homiletical snapshot, she identify the nature and content of the liturgical occasion in which the sermon

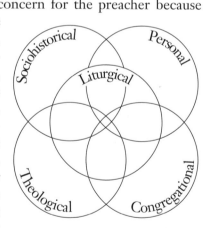

is to be embedded: Is this a regular congregational worship service, a wedding, a funeral, or some other occasion? What liturgical season is it? What is the tone of the music and liturgy? What lyrics will be sung and what prayers will be offered? Will the service include Eucharist or baptism?

6. The *conversational context*. Because the sermon participates fully in the matrix of congregational conversations instead of being set apart and

because the proclamatory conversation is grounded in the omnipresence of God, this context is not only central to the contextual understanding of choosing a snapshot of reality for the sermon, but it also encompasses all of the other contexts. Indeed, the range of congregational conversations grow out of and focus on the personal, congregational, theological, sociohistorical, and liturgical contexts. And the sermon both influences and is influenced by the congregational conversation in the same way that any utterance contributes to and is shaped by the whole of the conversation in which it is offered.

Conversations, however, are not static. As part of a congregational, conversational approach to proclamation, good preaching must be related to all six of these contexts, but especially to the constant evolution of the congregation's conversational, proclamatory engagement with all of the other contexts. The preacher must regularly ask, To what topics are various conversation circles attending? What topics are being ignored? Do the different conversations intersect or remain discrete? What conversations are new and exciting, old and stale, or slowly maturing?

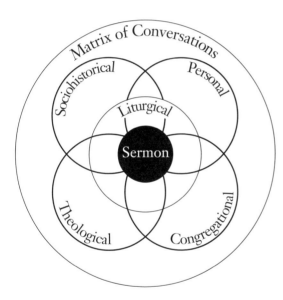

When preachers consider these six interrelated and overlapping contexts, they are able to enter the pulpit prepared to struggle with the question *"What is the most significant aspect or experience (i.e., snapshot) of God's hide-and-seek presence and its implications to which I can witness as a contribution to the conversation of this particular community at this particular moment?"*

Lens

The image of the preacher as photographer remains helpful in answering the above question. The photographer, using a trained eye, has a great deal of freedom in choosing and composing the subject of a snapshot but is nevertheless both limited and empowered by the photographic equipment. Specifically, for our purposes, we can say that the quality of the photograph depends on the quality and type of lens used.

For the preacher, the primary lens to be used to contribute to the congregational conversation is *Scripture*, and this choice of lens requires that the question itself be slightly reformulated: "What is the most significant aspect or experience (i.e., snapshot) of God's hide-and-seek presence and its implications to which I can witness *through the lens of Scripture* in conversation with this particular community on this particular occasion?"

In spite of the earlier move to shift the ground of this homiletical proposal away from Word-of-God theology and to the theological claim of divine omnipresence, this formulation of the question agrees with the Reformation assertion that preaching should be biblical. While postmodernism is suspicious of all claims of absolute authority, it values the particularity of well-defined perspectives. Thus the preacher need not suggest that other lenses are illegitimate in order to contribute to the proclamatory conversation specifically and unapologetically from the perspective of interpreting God's presence in the world through the Bible.

Nonetheless, the phrase "*through* the Bible" indicates a decisive break with the Reformation understanding of what it means to preach biblically and thus continues to break apart the practice of equating Bible and preaching with Christ as the Word of God. If the sixteenth-century Reformers had had access to photography as a metaphor for preaching, they would have claimed that a preacher points the camera lens *at* the Bible and takes a snapshot of it to show to the congregation.[17] To be relevant in today's postmodern world, however, biblical preaching must do more than just try to say what the Bible says. Indeed, biblical preaching must be more than an expository "updating" or "translating" of the ancient Bible for the modern era. The preacher should no longer simply hold the Bible in one hand and the newspaper in the other but should read the newspaper through a *biblical lens*. Scripture should no longer be viewed as the subject matter of the sermonic photograph. Instead, for Christians, the canon is the chosen lens by which God's presence in the world and the implications of that divine presence are viewed by the preacher and offered to the congregation.[18]

The Bible is, of course, accessible to all those who gather in the matrix of conversation circles, and the preacher can claim no monopoly of insight into it as a subject matter to be discussed or as a lens through which to view a particular issue. But while there is an ethic of egalitarian reciprocity around the conversation circle, asymmetry is also valued and sought after.

All conversation partners are equal *as persons*, but different kinds and levels of knowledge and experience are represented around the table. The preacher is not closer to God than others, may not have more life experience than others, and may not be as intelligent or wise as others. But he or she has been educated in biblical studies, and the congregation continues to set the preacher apart for the task of studying Scripture on their behalf. In other words, one of the most important gifts that the preacher brings to the proclamatory conversations of the church is expertise in academic, theological, and denominational approaches to biblical interpretation.

But preachers have more than just a primary lens through which to view God's presence. As photographers attach to their lenses teleconverters to increase the magnification power of the lens, and filters or flashes to influence the way the lens captures light, the preacher combines tradition with Scripture in composing a snapshot of God's presence in the world and in life. Scripture may be primary, but the knowledge and use of tradition is nevertheless an essential part of the specialized gift the preacher offers to the congregation's matrix of conversations. The preacher has no advantage over anyone else when it comes to experience or reason but has been trained as a specialist in Scripture and tradition on behalf of those who come together as the church to proclaim the gospel to one another.

Photo Album

If in any given liturgical occasion the preacher's task is to answer the question "What is the most significant aspect or experience of God's hide-and-seek presence and its implications to which I can witness through the lens of Scripture in conversation with this particular community on this particular occasion?" then yet another change in emphasis is called for in homiletics. If the sermon is not the Word of God, if it does not convey God's presence in a unique manner that other speech does not, then the great weight homileticians have placed on the individual sermon is overly burdensome. If preachers are essentially specialized conversation partners in the midst of many other conversation partners who both listen and speak, then the emphasis in our theology of preaching must shift from the "sermon event" to the preaching ministry.

It is little wonder that homileticians, who are perpetual guest preachers and who spend most of their time in the classroom trying to introduce beginning preachers to the task of developing and delivering sermons, have focused so much energy on what "*the* sermon" is and is supposed to do instead of what it means to preach in and to the same congregation every Sunday. One of the negative results of this emphasis on the sermon as a unique event is that those who also serve as pastor to the people to whom they preach expect too much of their sermons and are constantly disappointed with the effects of their preaching.[19] At the close of worship every Sunday, they stand in the doorway at the rear of the sanctuary waiting for a comment that lets them know whether the sermon confronted, comforted, challenged, or called anyone in any significant way. And, in truth, they are usually frustrated because they get "I enjoyed that sermon," followed by the succinct "Nice sermon, Pastor," followed by a statement about the temperature in the sanctuary more often than they get dramatic, substantive responses. But in a technological age when the members of the congregation are deluged by rhetoric from the moment they arise to when they go to bed, preachers should not realistically expect too much from a single fifteen to forty-five minute sermon.

Preachers must let go of the idea that they are carrying the weight of proclamation alone and view their preaching as contributing to a proclamatory conversation that both precedes and outlives any individual sermon. Once preachers recognize that their task is using their specialized training to point to God's presence in the myriad of life's experiences, then they can celebrate that while the individual sermon that profoundly changes lives is an occasional anomaly, one's preaching ministry that extends over weeks and months and years is part of a matrix of conversations that has an immeasurable influence on individuals' and the congregation's views of God, self, and the world. To return to our photography metaphor, one snapshot has but a minimal influence on the observer's view of the subject, but viewing a collection of artistic photographs can change one's perspective. Similarly, the single sermon rarely overturns the hearers' worldview. The *cumulative effect* of small, transforming conversions, however, makes the preaching ministry an immensely important part of the conversational proclamation ministry of the church. In preaching ministry, then, the individual snapshot offered in Sunday morning worship is only relatively significant in and of itself, just as it is rare that long-term Christians are "created" with dramatic altar calls following dramatic sermons. But the photo album of God's presence that the preacher keeps on the edge of the conversational roundtable responds to, builds on, enhances, and models the variety of utterances in which everyone proclaims their knowledge, experience, and interpretation of God-in-Christ, of God-in-the-world in such a way that authentic conversion can and does take place. It is one conversation/sermon after another that empowers persons to use Christian faith and traditions as a most significant resource in making meaning in today's postmodern environment.

Vocabulary Lessons

Now, a change in metaphors. Let's consider sermons as "vocabulary" lessons that use traditional Christian "language" to inform the matrix of conversations throughout the congregation and between the congregation and the world.[20]

In the twentieth century a "linguistic turn" in philosophy occurred in which explorations of the nature and power of language became a cornerstone to much philosophical reflection. Language came to be viewed not simply as referring to reality but as *determining* reality. A prime example is Kenneth Burke's assertion about language as a system of symbols:

> *Man is the symbol-using animal* [italics in the original]. . . . But can we bring ourselves to realize just what that formula implies, just how overwhelmingly much of what we mean by 'reality' has been built up for us through nothing but our symbol systems? Take away our books, and what little do we know about history, biography, even something so 'down to earth' as the relative position of the seas and continents? What is our 'reality' for today (beyond the paper-thin line of our own particular lives) but all this clutter of symbols about the past combined with whatever things we know mainly through maps, magazines, newspapers, and the like about the present? . . . and however important to us is the tiny sliver of reality each of has experienced firsthand, the whole overall 'picture' is but a construct of our symbol systems. To meditate on this fact until one sees its full implications is much like peering over the edge of things into an ultimate abyss. And doubtless that's one reason why, though man is typically the symbol-using animal, he clings to a kind of naïve verbal realism that refuses to realize the full extent of the role played by symbolicity in his notions of reality.[21]

Or consider the more succinct but ever more influential description of the nature and power of language offered by Martin Heidegger: "Language is the house of Being."[22]

Theology followed philosophy in this linguistic turn, and then homiletics followed theology. In a genealogy extending from Heidegger through the New Hermeneutic to the New Homiletic, the power of language to shape, define, and even create reality has become a mainstay of homiletical discussions. With a fair amount of ease, this understanding of the power and nature of language was merged with the Reformation understanding of the sermon as the Word of God. After all, did Paul not assert in Romans 10:17, "Faith comes from what is heard, and what is heard comes through the word of Christ."

Although I propose an alternative to the traditional view of preaching as the Word (with a capital W), this understanding of the power of language fits with the purpose of preaching that I am proposing. Pastors who preach week in and week out serve as *language teachers* who offer the "vocabulary" of Christian traditions to their congregations to use to shape, define, and create reality, that is, to make meaning of God, self, and the world. Indeed, there is a great need for such "vocabulary" lessons, given that congregations are generally biblically, doctrinally, and liturgically illiterate. As Thomas G. Long puts it,

> Another reason why Christian people are reticent about their faith in everyday settings is that they lack the necessary vocabulary. Without being romantically nostalgic about some golden past, we can acknowledge that there was a time when the common round of Christian folk possessed a basic theological and biblical vocabulary and knew, to some extent, how to use it. Words like grace, atonement, sin, and redemption were a more or less working vocabulary for people, at least church people, and they used them to make sense out of their lives. We speak often of biblical illiteracy, but even more pervasive is theological aphasia, the loss of theological speech. The biblical metaphors and theological categories have fallen away like the robes of royalty, and the vocabulary most readily at hand to describe ourselves, our world, and our deepest needs is the language of psychotherapy, or game playing, or human potential. The vocabulary of the faith, if employed at all, is used only to describe those experiences which are inward and private or conventionally religious. In other words, theological words are now not terms to be used to describe life; they have become words to be used to describe religion.[23]

When congregations are theologically illiterate, a great deal of energy in the pulpit must be spent on catechesis—in terms of reintroducing the theological "language" of the church to the church. Of course, in a postmodern setting, catechesis cannot properly be viewed as inducting seekers into the one, true understanding of the faith. Instead, catechesis is making Christian "language" readily available as a resource to those who are struggling to make meaning in and of the world. It is making traditional Christian "vocabulary" accessible to those striving to name and proclaim God's presence in their lives.

But language's power to create reality is more complex than is often assumed. Simply *encountering* new language will not create a new reality. When the preacher introduces new (or better, reintroduces old) "vocabulary" from Christian Scripture and traditions in a sermon, the hearers' world will not change instantaneously.

When I was in high school, we focused on vocabulary building. For four years in English classes, we used a series of vocabulary workbooks from which we learned ten words a week. I can remember what the workbooks looked like. I can remember matching the words and definitions on Mondays, filling in blanks in sentences on Tuesdays, writing out an original sentence using each word on Wednesday, writing a paragraph using all ten words on Thursdays, and taking vocabulary quizzes on Fridays. But I actually only remember learning a few words. That is not to say that I didn't learn many words; I just don't *remember* learning them. Most of them I assimilated into my vocabulary and use now without even being able to remember having learned them. The expanded vocabulary that was a result of this drawn-out process has expanded my world and my experience of the world. It gave me more tools to bring to my conversations about and with the world, to help me critically evaluate what I hear and what I say, and to make meaning in and of the world.[24] In other words, encountering new vocabulary for the first time rarely creates or transforms our reality. *Assimilation* of vocabulary into our language/symbol system does. It may be a minute transformation, but for a new word to become part of that vocabulary that gushes from our mouths without our searching for it is significant nevertheless. And, indeed, the more vocabulary assimilated, the more transformation that occurs.

The real power of the pulpit, therefore, lies less in the individual "vocabulary" lesson and more in the extended process of modeling the use of the "vocabulary" of Christian traditions Sunday after Sunday. It is lesson after lesson that effects assimilation. It takes time for the traditional "language" of ancient Christian communities to truly become the "language" of a citizen of the twenty-first century. It takes time for words and ideas like *prophecy*, *atonement*, *judgment*, *vocation*, *trinity*, and *Pentecost* to become words that one uses with the same ease that one speaks the words *tree*, *good*, *purple*, *Ireland*, and *anger*. It takes time for the biblical stories of creation, exodus, exile, incarnation, crucifixion, resurrection, and eschaton to become stories that one recounts with the same passion that one tells stories about grandparents and grandchildren. It takes time for the church's creeds and doctrines to become beliefs that are shared as comfortably as one expresses strong opinions about what was seen on the evening news last night. Indeed, it takes time for us to be able to name and describe God-in-Christ as God-with-us and as God-in-our-world with the same sense of assurance that we can name and describe relationships with family, friends, colleagues, or enemies. Christian "language" must become second nature if is to truly shape one's reality and identity. And such assimilation can only happen over time, especially since the "vocabulary" of Christian traditions involves not just words but metaphor, symbol, narrative, creed, ritual, poetry, music, and argument. Thus it should not be the primary goal of preachers to create and deliver memorable sermons in which parishioners remember "the Word" offered on that particular day.[25] Instead, analogous to language teachers, preachers model the use of the traditional theological "vocabulary" of Christian traditions Sunday after Sunday. Traditional terms, concepts, and stories must be repeated in the pulpit over time if preachers want them to become part of the hearers' reality.

But, with all due respect to Paul, it is not simply by hearing the Christian "language" that it becomes one's "language." It is by hearing and *speaking* the Christian "language" that it becomes one's own. It is through the expression of language that one builds his house of Being. It is by using symbols that he determines his reality. And, of course, his speaking implies someone else listening. In other words, it is by actively participating in proclamatory conversations that one assimilates the "language" of Christian traditions. Thus, the preacher's role is to provide the congregation with the Christian "vocabulary" that is necessary for any and all conversation in the church to be considered appropriately Christian.[26] While all those gathered around the table have equal claims to reason and to experience, the preacher has been specially trained in the "language" the church has inherited from Scripture and tradition. Preachers bring this special gift to the conversation circle as people struggle to proclaim God's hide-and-seek presence in the world and in their lives.

But, of course, language is not static, and assimilation of the traditional "language" of the faith does not imply that the ancient worldview or meta-narrative will or should be fully adopted. It is current use and not origins that ultimately determine a word's meaning. In conversation, therefore, there must be a great deal of negotiating what terms will mean. As difficult as it is for ancient Christian "language" to be claimed by an individual as one's own, it is even more complex for ancient Christian "language" to possess and be possessed by a community. Unless what I intend a word to mean and what you understand that word to mean coincides, we will end in confusion. In the end the two of us may disagree about the meaning of certain "vocabulary," but as long as we have clarity about our disagreement, we have the grounds for a converting conversation.

This means that while preachers may be "experts" in how the "vocabulary" of the faith was used in the past, they are on equal terms with everyone else concerning how the "vocabulary" is to be used in the present and future. They should certainly model in the pulpit not only remembering the church's "language" but re-membering it through critique and application in relation to the homiletical contexts described above. Nevertheless, it is when the "language" begins to be used by conversation partners other than the preacher as part of their proclamation of their experience, understanding, and interpretation of God, self, and the world and when its meanings are negotiated by those gathered in the conversation circle that it will be clear that assimilation is happening. It will be evident at this point that meaning is being made, that reality is being determined by the use of Christian "vocabulary." It will be evident that the preacher has been playing his or her proper role in the congregation's matrix of conversations. Having considered this role theologically, in the next chapter we will examine how the preacher is to fulfill this role throughout the course of sermon preparation and delivery.

Chapter 4

Practical Implications
of a Conversational Homiletic

No preacher would expect to communicate the whole of divine revelation in one sermon, though some have come perilously close to trying.

—Stuart Briscoe[1]

In chapter 3 I proposed a theology of preaching as a component of an ecclesiological theology of proclamation that represents a significant shift from traditional Protestant views of what occurs (or should occur) in the pulpit. Whether we are talking about older deductive approaches whose purpose is to convey a particular gospel truth or approaches of the New Homiletic in which sermons are formed to offer a specific experience of the gospel, these traditional views represent a funnel approach to preaching in which the Word of God incarnate in Jesus Christ is spoken (in some fashion) through Scripture, then through the preacher and to the congregation (and perhaps then by them to the world). In contrast I have argued that in a postmodern context Christian proclamation should be seen as the possession and responsibility not of the preacher but of the gathered community as the body of Christ. In give-and-take, persons struggle to make meaning of God, self, and the world; that is, they struggle to be mutually converted through conversation that uses Christian "language." In this approach the pulpit is not a lectern at center stage but a chair placed at the edge of the conversation table. From here the pastor participates in the congregation's matrix of proclamatory conversations by offering specialized knowledge of Christian Scriptures and traditions, pointing to the hide-and-seek presence of God in the world, and infusing the conversation with traditional, Christian theological "vocabulary" so that it might be assimilated, used, and critiqued by all participants.

In the material that follows, I discuss the implications of this conversational theology of proclamation and preaching for the practical tasks of planning, developing, and delivering sermons.

Same Time, Same Channel

In this conversational homiletic, there are two competing demands on preachers. The first is that any individual sermon, as an act of participating in the congregation's ongoing conversations, must be appropriate to the particular moment in the evolution of those conversations in which the sermon is offered. A poorly timed sermon is like a student raising his hand in class, but by the time he is called on the conversation has shifted and his comment has become irrelevant. Growing out of the congregation's proclamatory conversation instead of authoritatively setting the agenda for the conversation, preachers must always make sure their sermons fit and respond to the current state of that conversation's content, tone, and direction.

The second demand concerns the shift in emphasis from the individual sermon as a singular event to the ongoing preaching ministry. The preacher must actively participate in and be fully committed to the congregation's ongoing matrix of conversations. And in conversation, it is less any given individual utterance that has transforming power but more the cumulative effect of many utterances over time. Indeed, although it is rarely discussed in homiletical literature, all homileticians and preachers would recognize that it is preaching week in and week out that represents the fullest transforming power of the gospel.[2] In conversational terms, a consciously designed, extended preaching ministry plays a major role in the ongoing conversations in the congregation by effecting the gradual process of the assimilation of the "vocabulary" of the faith by individuals and within the community of theological discourse. With biblical, doctrinal, and historical illiteracy so high inside the church and so many voices in our culture competing for attention in the meaning-making process, the introduction of any specific element of Christian "vocabulary" in a single sermon is insufficient to the task of furthering the assimilation of the traditional "language" of the Christian faith to be used as a resource for making meaning in an ultimate sense. This second demand requires that one's sermons be interconnected over the course of one's preaching ministry in a congregation. In turn, the preacher must develop homiletical methods that will allow for the introduction, reinforcement, engagement, critique, and expansion of Christian doctrines, history, stories, poetry, logic, and prophecies in sermon after sermon.

In dealing with these two demands, the question is how to prepare sermons that are related over time but are nevertheless individually timely. While there is tension between the two demands, the individual sermonic occasion and the continual, cumulative effect of preaching should not be viewed as irreconcilably different entities but as two sides of the same homiletical coin. Preachers are not forced to choose allegiance to one over the other. They need not go either the route of beginning the sermon-writing process anew each Monday morning or developing a ten-part sermon series twelve months in advance. Indeed, not only is it possible to fulfill both demands, but it will be a powerful contribution to the church's tasking of doing conversational theology if preachers creatively prepare sermons that, on the one hand, build on one another week after week, year after year, and, on the other hand, fit the particular contexts in which they are spoken.

To combine the two demands and effectively fulfill them, preachers might begin to view the sermon development process as analogous to scriptwriting for a television series. Most weekly dramatic or situation-comedy television series strike a balance between two similar demands. On the one hand, there is continuity from show to show. Although new situations arise each week, the scriptwriters use a supply of regular main characters and settings that recur show after show. On the other hand, each individual episode is complete in and of itself; it has a story with a beginning, middle, and end; a plot with a conflict, rising action, and denouement.

While first-time or occasional viewers who tune in mid-season will miss nuances of the continuing elements of the series, they can usually follow the story line of the episode and "get something" out of or enjoy the show. If the continuing elements are too strong and overpower the individual nature of the episode, a first-time viewer may never tune in again, but if new or occasional viewers are able to follow the story, get to know the main characters fairly easily, and are stimulated or entertained by what they watch, they are more likely to begin watching more regularly. And as they become loyal viewers, they will gain more enjoyment from the series because they will become familiar with and more aware of continuing themes and developments. They watch as characters grow, relationships between characters develop, themes and issues repeat, and underlying sub-plots evolve. They will begin to get to know, develop relationships with, and identify with characters in some depth. They will begin conversing with other fans of the show about what happened last week and what they think will occur next week. And they may, at times, even find connections between their lives and story lines, issues, and quotes on the show.

To write a television series that meets the demands of creating a narrative world with coherence and gradual development over the course of the series and of creating an individual, complete narrative for each episode, television writers must constantly have their eyes focused on the details of the individual episode *and* have a vision for the broader sweep and flow of the series. And they must be attentive to how each influences the other, how each dictates limits and offers potential for the other. Were they in one episode to write action or dialogue that is "out of character," change the setting of the show for a single episode without sufficient explanation, or change the tone of the action or dialogue radically, they would break the coherence and stretch the credibility of the narrative world that the series has created over time. In contrast, slight changes in characterization, small shifts in setting, and little plot twists in individual episodes open up new directions for the series and are more easily accepted by the viewers. Knowing generally where and how they want the television series' season to end climatically allows the writers to build audience expectations and create surprises over a number of episodes. But the number of episodes available limits how far the writers can take the story world and the audience in a given season.

This analogy is flawed, of course, in that script writers are not part of a conversational community in the way that I am suggesting preachers should be and in that preaching is not oriented toward the task of entertaining. But the image does suggest an approach for supplementing the standard homiletical emphasis on the individual sermon with a concern for the ongoing role of the preaching ministry. As with script writing, preachers must have a bifocal approach to developing sermons—to preach effective individual sermons that cumulatively influence the community's proclamatory conversations and individuals' meaning-making processes. That is, they must move beyond the task of individual sermon preparation and on to the task of developing their preaching ministry (of which individual sermon preparation is a key part). They must think about biblical, theological, and imagistic continuity and diversity over time. They must ask how a particular sermon follows from recent sermons and flows into coming sermons. They must think not only about the design of a particular sermon but also about the flow and form of preaching over a number of weeks and months and years. They must design sermons that meet the needs of regular conversation partners and are at the same time inviting to occasional worship attendees.

Balancing the calls for continuity and timeliness in preaching requires preachers to keep two sets of questions ever before them. The first set concerns the role the individual sermon plays in responding to the current state of the congregation's matrix of proclamatory conversations. Here the preacher should ask the following types of questions during sermon preparation:

- *In this sermon how will I respond to what I have been hearing in the congregation's conversations?* Will I express consent or disagreement? Will I continue down the path of the conversation or try to change the direction of the conversation? Will I broaden or narrow the focus of some aspect of the conversation? Are there problems in the conversation itself (in terms of the ethics and etiquette of the community) that need to be addressed?

- *Which particular conversation partners am I addressing or responding to most directly in this sermon?* Is there a conversation that involves the whole congregation and to which I wish to contribute in this sermon? Am I speaking to the whole congregation as a matrix of conversations and looking to bring together elements of concern/interest that stretch across the matrix? Or is there some particular conversation circle I wish to open to the broader congregation and to address?

- *What should be the nature and tone of my sermonic contribution to the conversation?* Am I providing background information related to some conversational topic in a didactic manner? Am I sharing personal testimony or experiences related to the topic? Am I describing or prescribing behavior? Am I tentatively proposing a new interpretation of something or strongly asserting a traditional interpretation? Do I want to offer theological content or spiritual experience? Am I constructing or deconstructing? Do I wish to introduce a matter into the conversation or probe more deeply into a matter that is already familiar to the congregation and a part of the conversation? What has the tone of the conversation been and do I want to keep that tone or alter it?

- *What should the function of the sermon be in relation to the state of the conversation?* Does the state of the conversation lend itself to an evangelistic call for personal repentance, or for a prophetic call to social action by the community as a whole? Have there been elements in the conversation that call for pastoral attention to offering comfort and assurance? Has confusion about elements of the theological, biblical, liturgical, or ecclesial traditions been expressed that need explanation and clarification? Is there a need to raise doubts so that the conversation can be opened to wider understandings and interpretations of God's presence?

By keeping these sorts of questions in front of themselves, preachers will make sure their sermons are always appropriate to the current and changing state of the congregation's conversation.

But pastors must also make sure their sermons work cumulatively over time to influence the matrix of conversations and help fund the postmodern process of making meaning by supplying Christian "vocabulary" to be assimilated. To do that they must also keep a second set of questions before themselves as they develop their preaching ministry:

- *How does a particular individual sermon relate to other sermons I have preached recently or will preach soon?* Does this sermon flow out of previous sermons or turn in a new direction? Does this sermon foreshadow sermons to come or does it draw to a close a progression of sermons unconnected from what will come on the following Sunday? Does the sermon come at the beginning, middle, or end of a chain of connected sermons (and how are they connected)? Does the focus of the sermon build on previous and/or lead into future statements, questions, and themes of sermons? How is the biblical text for this sermon related to those of nearby sermons (lectionary, *lectio continua*, etc.)? Is there a repetition or progression of doctrinal, ethical, or existential issues explored? Does the sermon echo or expand previous imagery and language; will the imagery and language lead to the creation of related imagery and language in sermons to come? Are the emotions the preacher invites the congregation to experience this week the same as, similar to, or different from the preceding and following Sundays?
- *How does this sermon relate to other sermons I have preached or will preach that deal with the same element of the Christian "vocabulary"?* When and how have I preached on this theme, question, doctrine, experience, or biblical text before, and when and how will I again? When else have I preached or will I preach on things *related to* the theme, question, doctrine, experience, or biblical text before, and when and how will I again? How did I deal with this liturgical occasion last time it occurred; what should I do similarly this time; and what should I do differently?

By keeping questions like these before them, preachers will make sure their sermons work together to aid the congregation in their assimilation of Christian "vocabulary" as they struggle to make meaning in a conversational manner.

It will now be helpful to examine the tasks and concerns discussed in most standard homiletical literature as they relate to a cumulative approach to preaching.

Choosing Biblical Texts

I noted earlier that in discussing sermon preparation, most homileticians deal almost exclusively with the individual sermon. The one exception is when textbooks deal with choosing biblical texts for sermons. In this instance, three basic options are usually discussed: 1) a denominational or ecumenical lectionary (*lectio selecta*), 2) continuous readings (*lectio continua*), and 3) the weekly selection of texts without a specific overarching plan. There are pros and cons to each of these three approaches. My interest, however, is in discussing these options in relation to our conversational homiletic and our need to offer a sermon that is both appropriate to the current state of a congregation's conversation and responsive to the demand for continuity.

The Lectionary

Using a selected lectionary in worship offers much to one who wishes to preach cumulatively. Lectionaries are based on the liturgical year, which revolves around the story of, existential encounter with, and doctrines related to the Christ event from Jesus' birth to Pentecost. Cycling through the liturgical calendar and the texts prescribed for the seasons each year does much to invite the congregation's assimilation of a great deal of the basic "vocabulary" of Christian traditions. Moreover, since lectionaries generally assign four biblical readings—from the Hebrew Bible, Psalms, Epistles, and Gospels for each Sunday (with some variation at different times of the year)—and works on a three-year cycle, a wider range of biblical stories, prophetic texts, poetry, and discourse is introduced into the congregation's conversation than in the other two methods of choosing texts. And, finally, since lectionaries are denominationally or ecumenically defined, the congregation's conversation has a natural bridge to other congregations' conversations following the liturgical calendar and using the same or similar lectionaries.

There are disadvantages to using the lectionary approach, however. Lectionary texts are based more on loyalty to the liturgical calendar than to the biblical writings. This means that the connection from week to week and year to year will be more in terms of liturgical themes than scriptural continuity. While this approach aids in combating some elements of illiteracy concerning the worshiping and doctrinal traditions of a congregation, doctrinal themes that play little role in liturgical development receive short shrift and little aid is given to overcoming scriptural illiteracy. Indeed, discontinuity between scriptural texts on a week-to-week basis for lectionary users is heightened by the fact that while all four prescribed lessons may be read in worship, preachers cannot preach (or at least cannot preach well) on all four texts for a given Sunday. While reading Scripture in worship does more than just provide the basis for the sermon and indeed is itself a part of the congregation's matrix of proclamatory conversations, reading lessons as part of the liturgy alone will probably not inform the congregation's conversation at a deep level. Achieving that depth will require struggling with the text publicly, and to struggle with Scripture well in worship, *one* text from the lectionary must be chosen as the basis of the sermon (with, perhaps, some of the others playing a subordinate role). To be as appropriate as possible to the current state of the conversation, the preacher may choose a text from the Hebrew Bible this week, a Gospel text next week, and an epistle text after that. And even with the choice of four texts, the readings may seem to have little to do with the content and tone of the matrix of conversations on that given Sunday.

Continuous Reading

In the continuous reading approach to choosing texts for sermons, preachers work their way through a biblical writing or a section of a writing over the course of a number of Sundays. (Contemporary lectionaries contain elements of the continuous reading plan, especially in Ordinary Time.) This may involve reading every verse of the particular writing over time or choosing representative passages throughout a biblical book. The advantages to this approach are similar to using the lectionary in that its strength is in relation to the cumulative demand. Whereas the cumulative effect of the lectionary is rooted in the liturgical year, however, the cumulative effect of the continuous reading model is scripturally determined. Preaching through Genesis or Isaiah or Mark or Galatians provides continuity week after week and will help the congregation assimilate a biblical writer's unique "vocabulary."

The problem, of course, is that this is a slow approach to dealing with the canon as a whole. Moreover, examining the theological and existential content and point of view of one writer means ignoring other biblical voices. Certainly, lectionaries have their own canon within a canon, but it tends to be broader than is allowed with continuous reading. Another disadvantage with this approach is, as with the lectionary, that a long-term plan of continuous readings may have little to do with issues and topics currently being discussed in the rest of the matrix of conversations.

Individual Choice

Finally, there is the option in which preachers personally choose the biblical passage for the sermon on any given Sunday. Texts are usually chosen on the basis of themes or topics. This model has the advantage of great flexibility and allows the preacher to choose a text each week that is especially relevant to a current aspect of the congregation's matrix of conversation.

The disadvantage, however, is that continuity from Sunday to Sunday depends completely on the preacher. Whereas continuous reading and lectionary approaches push the preacher to re-member—to recall and to piece together again in a meaningful way—for the congregation a wide array of elements of the Christian traditions, individual choice means that while there may be thematic connection from one week to the next, the element re-membered for the congregation will be parts the preacher remembers. In other words, in this approach preachers contribute to the conversations only those elements of Christian "vocabulary" they have already assimilated. Having complete control over the choice of texts will not push preachers, or their congregations, to struggle with the limitations of the preacher's mastery of Christian "language."

Clearly, none of these three plans is perfect, and none is totally flawed. Each has strengths and weaknesses for a conversational approach to preaching. Any one of them or combination of them could be used to meet demands of preaching over time and preaching in the moment. Three broad guidelines for choosing texts for conversational preaching can, in fact, be adapted to whichever approach a preacher prefers.

1. Texts should relate to the core of the congregation's conversation. It is important to recognize that while conversations are to a degree free-flowing, they also have some structure and amorphous thematic centers. These structures and centers change more slowly than the immediate content of the conversation. For a sermon to be relevant to an ongoing conversation, sermons need not speak to *exactly* what was said in, for instance,

a Wednesday evening study group but rather to the broad themes focused on and structures used by the conversational circle. Preachers, therefore, should usually select texts that relate to the core of a congregation's conversation and only occasionally choose ones that deal with the details of the conversation.

2. At times, texts should not respond to the current state of the conversation so much as move the conversation in new directions. While I have argued that the church's proclamatory conversations should not focus on what is said from the pulpit, this does not mean that what is said in the pulpit should never be designed to start a new conversation or change the direction of an ongoing conversation. So sermon preparation can be responsive to the current state of the conversation without simply looking for a way each week to react to that current state. This means that often texts should be chosen because they introduce something new into the conversational matrix. By introducing new biblical "vocabulary" into the conversation, the preacher helps refocus the congregation's evolving struggles to make meaning of God, self, and the world.

3. Texts should be chosen for more than one Sunday at a time. This practice not only enables other worship planners to coordinate music, liturgy, and preaching, but it also brings continuity and progress into sermon preparation. Choosing a group of texts in advance means that the coordination of texts with conversations in the church will be somewhat loose, and this is the way it should be at this early point in the preparation process. Preachers will not know in advance what will be said in conversations or what conversations will arise spontaneously, but they should know what conversations are planned in various conversation circles of the church as well as which are ongoing and central to the life and proclamation of the community and which are peripheral. The level of knowledge of the present and future conversation of the community that is required for one to be a good steward of the matrix of conversations while choosing biblical texts means that while advance preparation is called for, sermon planning should not be done too far in advance. To plan too far in advance implies that preaching is at the center of the church's proclamation and that the conversation should conform to it. If preaching is, instead, a significant, specialized, cumulative contribution to the congregation's ongoing, proclamatory conversation, then choosing texts should occur only a couple of months, liturgical seasons, or thematic or textual series in advance. Preachers who follow the lectionary can choose the texts on which the sermon will focus for a liturgical season at a time. Those who plan to use continuous readings can select the biblical writing to be used

and determine how many weeks will be given to the writing (and, if representative passages are to be used to work through the writing as opposed to every verse being dealt with, which passages). And those who choose individually can choose a set of readings at a time, greatly increasing the level of continuity of this option.

Biblical Interpretation for Conversational Preaching

Exegesis is basically a process of asking questions of a biblical text. Although the origin of historical criticism is the Enlightenment pursuit of scientific, objective knowledge of the Bible and the history behind its texts, it is commonly recognized that any act of interpretation is by its very nature a subjective act. Exegetes can never remove themselves from the interpretive equation. Interpreters can never step out of their sociohistorical context and the worldviews that context embraces and interpret the text fully on its own terms. Interpreters can never get back to the texts and the history related to them completely anew, as if contemporary interpretation is not influenced by the fact that the texts have been interpreted for two thousand years.

And most important for our purposes, interpretation is influenced by the purpose for which one is interpreting in the first place. The destination prejudices one in choosing a route for the journey. This is inescapable, but not necessarily negative. In other words, the kinds of questions interpreters ask in exegesis are fundamentally determined by the kinds of answers they hope to discover about the texts and by interpreters' conceptions of the audiences on behalf of which they are asking the questions in the first place. A secular historian who studies a biblical text in order to present research results in writing to an academic guild will ask different questions and thus find different understandings of that text than will a pastor who studies a text in preparation for a sermon. Different theologies of preaching and different views of those to whom one is preaching will also cause one to look for different kinds of understandings and thus ask different sorts of questions of a text in sermon preparation. Fundamentalist pastors who view preaching as the passing on of the inerrant Word of God found in Scriptures will ask different questions of the text than will liberation-oriented pastors who seek to use the Bible to fund a call to acts of peace and justice. Guest evangelists who turn to a text to shape a sermon that ends in an invitation to repentance and dedication will seek different answers and thus ask different questions of a text than a pastor who is shaping a sermon to comfort a congregation that is in the midst of an emotional and spiritual crisis.

This by no means implies that interpreters should abandon textual, historical, sociological, source, intertextual, form, rhetorical, redaction, literary, theological, and ideological types of criticism. Instead, these approaches to asking questions of a biblical text, which are shared by different interpreters with different purposes, are controlled and let loose, limited and stretched, by the particular goal and its broad, overarching questions that led the individual to the process of interpretation in the first place. The matter before us, then, is not to review the different exegetical methodologies available to the preacher but to examine the broad, overarching questions that should shape the exegetical process of preachers who stand in the pulpit to offer a monological contribution to their congregation's ongoing matrix of conversations proclaiming God's hide-and-seek presence in the world and the implications of that divine presence for making meaning of God, self, and the world.

In chapter 3, I offered the metaphor of preachers as photographers using Scripture as a lens through which to take a snapshot of God's presence in the world. This model implies that we who read Scripture as part of our journey to the conversational pulpit do not interpret the text for its own sake. We ask questions of the text not primarily to offer an interpretation of that text to the congregation (although that may be a part of the sermon itself) but to focus our interpretation on God in the world and life. We ultimately perform exegesis not to get a better view *of* the text but to get a better view *through* the text. This looking *through* instead of *at* the text means, however, that we must look all the more carefully *into* the text. It is rarely on the surface of the biblical text that we will catch a significant glimpse of God's presence in today's world. One must use critical exegetical methods to dig deep into the layers of meaning in the text if one hopes the text will be a useful lens for those making meaning in a give-and-take conversational manner today.

The difference between the more traditional exegetical approach of looking *at* the text and this proposal for looking *through* the text can be demonstrated in relation to biblical texts that might otherwise be passed over by a preacher. In a homiletic where the preacher's role is essentially to proclaim what the text says or the experience it offers, texts that dehumanize women, promote slavery, justify violence, negatively stereotype anyone who is other, or make God look capricious offer only offensive messages. If the preacher's role, however, is to use biblical texts to look at the human condition as it manifests itself today and at the implications that God's presence in today's world has for our understanding and addressing of that condition, then texts whose surface-level message is theologically offensive may serve well as lenses for conversing about difficult issues we might otherwise avoid in the pulpit—that is, as long as we don't assume the text has the last say on the issue, that it is the final voice in the conversation.

The goal of using a biblical text as a lens to focus the preacher's snapshot of God's hide-and-seek presence in the world profoundly shapes the way exegesis is performed. But more is still to be said on the matter. The fact that the preacher's snapshot is to be offered as a contribution to an ongoing congregational conversation also significantly influences the process of exegesis. Preachers study the text with the conversational context narrowing (or broadening) what one looks for in the text. In other words, at different points in the congregation's conversational life, a particular biblical text might be used in a range of ways to enhance and advance the conversation. As preachers study a text for a given Sunday, they must ask, "What do I see through this lens that would make an appropriate contribution to our conversation?" Or to mix our metaphors, at issue is what "vocabulary" the text offers, suggests, or relates to that is appropriate to bring into the current state of the conversation. There may be many good sermons for any preacher to develop in relation to any given biblical text, but writing one that is appropriate to the state of the conversation is the task at hand. We must ask, What Christian "vocabulary" can I re-member from my struggle with this text in order to aid the congregation in their mutually converting, conversational proclamation?

But, of course, paired with the demand that the exegesis be directed toward the immediate needs of the congregation's conversation is the demand that sermons work together cumulatively to aid the ongoing matrix of conversations. Preachers must ask exegetical questions of a text that grow, in part, out of the homiletical questions of how this week's sermon will relate to last week's and next week's sermon, how this week's sermon will relate to snapshots of God's presence, and how the re-membering of Christian "vocabulary" contributed to the conversation at times more distant. In other words, exegesis is shaped by the question, What do I see of God's presence in the world through this text that relates to what I contributed to the conversation recently and will contribute soon? And what "vocabulary" is suggested by this text that relates "vocabulary" I have offered to the conversation at earlier times and will again some time?

Sermonic Form

During the last thirty years or so, homiletical scholarship has revolved, to a great deal, around the question of sermonic form. It is an important issue since, as homileticians point out, the form of preaching implies a certain theological understanding of the nature of the Good News and Scripture and, conversely, certain theological understandings of the nature of the Good News and Scripture suggest certain preaching forms. The question before us is, then, what kind of sermon form is implied by this conversational ecclesiology and homiletic? This question is especially interesting, since I began this work by rejecting what would seem on the surface to be the obvious answer: that is, that a conversational theology of proclamation calls for sermons that use actual conversation during worship. Since dialogue sermons do not represent true, egalitarian conversation in which mutual conversion can slowly and progressively take place, I have argued that sermons best remain monological contributions to an ongoing congregational matrix of proclamatory conversations. So what monological sermon form is implied by this understanding of proclamation as the possession and responsibility of the community of theological discourse as a whole? What kind of expression, what flow of thought and images, what rhetorical structures are implied by a conversational homiletic?

The answer is that there isn't one . . . there are many. In conversation, no one form of speech is appropriate at all times. In conversation, meaning is not simply being conveyed from a speaker to a listener. Meaning is being made in give-and-take fashion by all conversation partners who share the roles of both speakers and listeners. As meaning is negotiated and grappled with, many speech forms are called for. At one point we make an assertion. At another we raise a question. Then we offer a statement of agreement only to follow up with a challenge. We may speak our own mind one moment and quote an "authority" the next. Sometimes response may call for a personal anecdote while another requires a logical, even syllogistic attempt to explore an issue. At times we will need to unpack observations by breaking them apart into multiple subpoints, while a short analogy or powerful metaphor will do at others.

Because the preacher stands in the pulpit to offer a contribution to an ongoing congregational conversation, no one sermon form will be appropriate week in and week out. On different Sundays, he or she will choose to make different sorts of contributions to the constantly changing conversations in the church. At times a didactic, three-point sermon will be more appropriate than an experiential-oriented, narrative sermon. It is not correct to assume that by simply changing content, one or two basic sermon forms will serve every occasion. The preacher needs a multitude of sermon forms that can be used and adapted.[3]

One of the reasons many preachers avoid embracing multiple forms for their own preaching may be the mistaken equation of style and voice in popular homiletical parlance. In scholarly homiletical circles, style is used literally while voice is used metaphorically. That is, style is a rhetorical term and refers to the manner in which one speaks while in the pulpit—the form of the sermon, the speed and rhythm of speech. Voice, in contrast, is a psycho-socio-theological term. At a literal level, voice is simply the sound that humans make when they speak. As with fingerprints, each individual has a unique voice—unique in tonal quality, pitch, pronunciation—caused by air passing through the vocal cords, over the tongue, across the teeth, and through the lips. At this literal level, voice is an element of style that is very much an issue in public speaking. But rarely are homileticians today referring to this literal level when speaking of voice. Homiletical use of the metaphor of voice has been influenced especially by feminist studies of girls and women devoiced in and by patriarchal society.[4] Throughout most of Christian history, this devoicing meant silencing in that women were not allowed to preach. As women claimed their right and call to stand in and speak from the pulpit in the twentieth century, devoicing meant that women preachers were told that they did not sound like a preacher—that is, did not sound like a *male* preacher (a literal voice issue)—and that they should imitate men in the pulpit. Feminist studies in and of preaching, however, began to argue that women had something different to offer in the pulpit than men do. Women have a different "voice" than men do.[5] Out of these struggles by women called to a ministry so long dominated by men has grown the common homiletical recognition that every preacher needs to find her or his own unique voice, not just the way she or he is going to speak in the pulpit, but *who* she or he is going to be in the pulpit.[6] The question of voice is asked as "How do I bring all of the things that make me who I am (gender, age, race, family history, education, class, theology, emotional experiences, ideologies, social relationships) to bear on the task of preaching?"

Thus voice and style are related but not synonymous. Preachers should certainly use different styles of preaching in a regular Sunday service, an evangelistic revival, and a funeral, but will preach with the same voice in all. So preachers need to learn to use different styles and forms of preaching to carry their voice appropriately in different preaching occasions. Or, more to the point for this proposal, preachers need to master different styles and forms of preaching to carry their voice appropriately at different moments in the congregation's conversational life together.

But we can be yet more specific about the need for a variety of sermonic forms in relation to a conversational homiletic. A great deal of the academic discussion of sermon form in homiletics has dealt with the choice between deductive and inductive preaching. Deductive sermon movement has been greatly chastised since the rise of the New Homiletic in the 1970s, and not without reason. Since the Middle Ages, multiple- (usually three-) point sermons meant to break open a central theological topic or element of a scriptural passage have dominated pulpit practice. But rarely do people actually engage the world and learn and grow in this deductive-logical manner. Indeed, with the rise of electronic media (especially television), people have a more difficult time listening to detailed, logical arguments meant to persuade in the style of classical rhetoric. Inductive sermonic approaches, it is argued, are more appropriate to the way people come to know and believe in anything in our modern, technological age. The reasoning is that in everyday meaning-making processes, people are usually moving from particular experiences, observations, and thoughts to general conclusions instead of moving from general truth claims to particular implications and applications. Therefore, to be as effective as possible and true to human experience, sermons should use inductive logic.

If we are honest, however, we must recognize that human thought constantly mixes deductive and inductive reasoning. Indeed, in real life, they two form a reasoning circle (not necessarily circular reasoning) in which conclusions reached through inductive reasoning become the starting point for deductive reasoning. And, likewise, implications derived deductively from strongly held truth claims become the building blocks of inductive reasoning that leads to new conclusions.[7] Thus to be true to the full range of human experience, preachers should be able and willing to use both inductive and deductive approaches in sermons.

More important for our purposes, we must recognize that conversation as a whole works inductively, moving from the particular to the general. Those participating in a conversation draw general conclusions (make meaning) by piecing together individual expressions offered by different conversation partners (including themselves) over the course of time. But while the conversational process is primarily inductive, this process is funded by a range of inductive and deductive contributions as described above. Thus, as a significant contribution to the congregation's conversation, a preacher's preaching ministry should evidence a broad inductive movement, but individual sermons will need to vary between diverse deductive and inductive forms if they are effectively to engage the particular state of the conversation at different times.

Imagery

The scope of this project does not allow me to discuss different types of sermon "illustrations," such as stories, figurative language, quotations, contemporary events, personal accounts, examples, and humor. Because these types of language help construct the snapshot (image) of God's hide-and-seek presence in the world that the preacher wants to offer the congregation instead of simply illustrating a point, I use the term *imagery* to encompass them all. My concern is not with homiletical use of imagery in general, but with how a conversational homiletic changes the way preachers approach the use of imagery. Specifically, we need to consider how the double demand that sermons work both cumulatively and in the conversational moment influences our use of imagery.

Usually homiletical writers discuss imagery simply in relation to its appropriateness to the sermon of which it is a part. For example, David Buttrick suggests three criteria to determine the appropriateness of imagery for a sermon:

1. There must be a clear analogy between an idea in sermon content and some aspect of the illustration.
2. There ought to be a parallel between the structure of content and the shape of an illustration.
3. The illustration should be "appropriate" to the content (i.e., it should share much the same moral, aesthetic, or social value as the idea being illustrated).[8]

These are helpful and necessary criteria. But because they deal with the sermon only in relationship to itself (and its content), they do not go far enough in testing the appropriateness of imagery in relation to the congregation's conversation or to other sermons.

For preaching to work cumulatively in aiding proclamatory conversation partners to assimilate Christian "vocabulary," we must ask how imagery in a sermon works with imagery in other sermons we have preached and will preach to make a specific element of Christian "vocabulary" available and usable by the hearers. We should seek not imagery that will be memorable (although it may be memorable) but imagery that can be acquired and adapted by others as they make Christian "vocabulary" their own. As I have said, this process takes time, so one must look for and create imagery for a sermon that works with (e.g., shares continuity with, elaborates, expands) imagery used at other times. This means that there is a need for the balanced use of both reverberation and diversity of imagery. By *reverberation* I mean imagery that evokes and echoes imagery and ideas offered at other times without simply repeating that imagery (although this may at times be useful as well). For example, I have used story-sermons, in which the whole sermon is a narrative, as an important element of my preaching ministry. Because these sermons are occasional and share similar structural approaches to God's hide-and-seek presence in the world, I decided it was also important that they share some common elements, such as narrator and setting.[9] In this way the story-sermons reverberate with one another but do not simply repeat what I offered before. Listeners begin to find a level of comfort not only with the narrative form of the sermons but also with their narrative world. They remember less the individual stories than the basic view of the world and the Christian life the stories as a group portray. Indeed, in discussion of these sermons, I have been pleased to hear parishioners mingle elements from different stories into a single recollection, for the imagery we use throughout our preaching ministry should work cumulatively as a resource for the congregation's process of meaning making—the imagery we offer in our contributions to the conversations should become part of the mosaic of imagery and ideas they offer to the conversations.

Preachers must also use a wide *diversity* of images over time in order to give people the opportunity to engage Christian "vocabulary" from many different angles and encourage the expansion of the experiential, emotional, and intellectual horizons of all those participating in the conversation: imagery from diverse social categories: class, ethnicity, age, single/partnered/married, educational level, religion; imagery from nature, business, the church, art, world events; imagery from poetry, music, television, fiction, newspapers, Scripture, movies; imagery that evokes joy, praise, empathy, sadness, awe, puzzlement, anxiety, penitence, pride, resolve, quietness. The point is straightforward: the more varied the imagery in preaching, the more listeners will take Christian "vocabulary" seriously as an element of their conversations that make meaning of God, self, and world.

Putting It All Together

I have discussed different aspects of sermon development—choosing biblical texts, doing exegesis, developing sermon form, incorporating imagery—in relation to the demands to have a preaching ministry in which sermons work together cumulatively and to offer individual sermons that are appropriate contributions to the current state of the congregation's proclamatory conversation. This examination has moved us a significant distance away from focusing on sermon development solely to the development of a cumulative preaching ministry. What remains to be discussed is a *preaching-ministry preparation process* by which these different components are brought together in the regular work of the preacher so that attention given to preaching over time strengthens the offering of the individual sermon and individual sermons strengthen the preacher's cumulative contribution to the congregation's ongoing matrix of conversations.

Let's consider two possible processes.[10] Both break apart the tasks of sermon preparation that are often described in terms of a one-week schedule and extend them over weeks and months.[11] I have already recommended that biblical texts for sermons should be chosen in groups several months or liturgical seasons in advance in order to begin thinking about sermons in groups instead of individually. If the other developmental steps are moved back a few weeks before the date the individual sermon is to be delivered, the steps of preparation for one sermon can overlap with those for other sermons. Let's consider five steps as the basic building blocks of sermon preparation:

1. Choosing a biblical text
2. Interpreting the biblical text
3. Developing a sermonic focus
4. Developing imagery for the sermon
5. Developing the sermon as a whole

If these steps are extended over a number of weeks instead of being compressed into one week, and if preachers connect the sermon preparation of a number of sermons, the cumulative approach to the preaching ministry becomes, in part, secondhand, simply by the fact that preachers are thinking about more than one sermon at a time.

This extension of the sermon preparation process may seem quite daunting at first, especially since so many of us approach sermon preparation in a one-track fashion, one step at a time for one sermon at a time. A significant problem with this approach, however, is that the sermons offered to the congregation reflect this disconnected process. Each sermon is an individual speech event that is barely related to what was preached the week before or what will be preached the week after. Preachers must develop a process in which they are working on numerous sermons at a time if integration from week to week is to occur. In fact, this sort of multitasking is part of the way we operate in most other areas of our life. For example, in seminary, we study several subjects at a time and have overlapping responsibilities for each class—class attendance, reading assignments, test preparation, papers, and presentations. By overlapping such a diversity of tasks and subjects in the course of a single term, students are naturally pushed to reflect on and integrate the connections between, for example, the thesis of a lecture in ethics, the issues being tested in a midterm for a class in church history, observations being made during research for an exegesis paper in a course on Genesis, and the claims found in a textbook being read for a class in Christology. The same type of reflection and integration will occur if preachers develop a process by which the work on different sermons is performed in overlapping stages. Although switching from sermon preparation mode to a preaching ministry process may be awkward at first, it will lead us to the establishment of a rhythm in both the preparation process and in the preaching in worship that will become easier to maintain than scurrying each Monday to start from scratch to find a message for the coming Sunday. The difference in result will be like the difference between a person playing solos on a snare drum, a bass drum, and cymbals sequentially and a person joining a jam session by playing a drum set where one foot keeps the main beat on the bass drum, the other foot keeps the off beat on the hi-hat cymbals, the right hand establishes the flowing rhythm, and the left hand adds an element of syncopation . . . all at the same time.

It is also important to emphasize that the proposals that follow are suggestive rather than prescriptive. I present two possibilities but focus on the second one, for I think it holds more potential for creating a cumulative homiletic. All preachers, however, must find their own pattern and time line for working on their preaching. And, indeed, the proposals are linear descriptions of a creative process that is actually quite fluid. But disciplined management of time in general is an aid, not a hindrance, to artistic and theological creativity. In sum, the processes offered here should simply be viewed as *examples* of processes of preaching/sermon preparation that one can adapt to the rhythm of one's own conversational community and individual life of study. Thus while these processes may work fairly well for some readers, for others it may be less the details of what follows and more the basic approach that the proposals illustrate that is helpful. What is most important is for each preacher to find a process that moves beyond focusing on individual sermons to one that gives proper attention to individual sermons in the context of attending to the connections among sermon after sermon after sermon.

Grouping Tasks

One process by which preachers can relate preparation for different sermons is simply to do the same step of sermon preparation for a number of sermons at the same time. Instead of spreading sermon preparation out through the course of the week, preachers can set aside one day of the week in which to retreat into one of the sermon preparation tasks for longer periods of time. For example, as shown in table 1, the pattern of preparation for preaching during an individual liturgical season would look something like this:

- Two or three months before the season begins, the preacher chooses the biblical texts for the entire season.
- Five or six weeks before the season begins, the preacher spends a day performing exegesis on all of the selected passages.
- Two to four weeks before the season begins, the preacher returns to the exegetical work, chooses foci (i.e., the basic snapshots or elements of Christian "vocabulary" to be contributed to the conversation) for all of the sermons, and begins brainstorming about imagery and perhaps sermonic forms to be used.
- Once the season begins, the preacher spends one day or so each week pulling together all of the work done so far into a sermon for the coming Sunday.

By thinking about preaching during a liturgical season as a whole but then doing the final stage of sermon preparation individually, the preacher will offer sermons to the congregation that fit the current state of its conversations and at the same time work together to build a cumulative contribution to the ongoing conversations of the church.

Moreover, the sermons within a particular season or series of sermons will be related not only to one another but also to sermons offered during the preceding and following seasons or series, since the advanced

Week beginning on	Finish developing sermon for	Pre-Writing tasks
		TABLE 1
Pentecost 16	Pentecost 17	Choose texts for *Advent*-Christmas
Pentecost 17	Pentecost 18	
Pentecost 18	Pentecost 19	Exegesis for *Advent*-Christmas
Pentecost 19	Pentecost 20	
Pentecost 20	Pentecost 21	Choose texts for Epiphany
Pentecost 21	Pentecost 22	Develop foci and imagery for *Advent*-Xmas
Pentecost 22	Reign of Christ	
Reign of Christ	Advent 1	
Advent 1	*Advent 2*	Exegesis for Epiphany
Advent 2	Advent 3	
Advent 3	Advent 4	Develop foci and imagery for Epiphany
Advent 4	Xmas 1	
Xmas 1	Epiphany	
Epiphany	Baptism	Choose texts for Lent
Baptism	Epiphany 2	
Epiphany 2	Epiphany 3	
Epiphany 3	Epiphany 4	Exegesis for Lent
Epiphany 4	Epiphany 5	
Epiphany 5	Epiphany 6	Develop foci and imagery for Lent
Epiphany 6	Transfiguration	Choose texts for Easter
Transfiguration	Lent 1	
Lent 1	Lent 2	
Lent 2	Lent 3	Exegesis for Easter
Lent 3	Lent 4	
Lent 4	Lent 5	Develop foci and imagery for Easter
Lent 5	Palm/Passion	Choose texts for early Ordinary Time
Palm/Passion	Easter Sunday	
Easter Sunday	Easter 2	
Easter 2	Easter 3	
Easter 3	Easter 4	Exegesis for early Ordinary Time
Easter 4	Easter 5	
Easter 5	Easter 6	Develop foci and imagery for early Ordinary Time
Easter 6	Ascension	
Ascension	Pentecost	
Pentecost		

sermon-preparation days will overlap them. We can see this illustrated by following the sermon preparation for the Second Sunday of Advent, which is highlighted in italics in table 1. The text for Advent 2 is chosen and interpreted along with the other Advent and Christmas texts during Ordinary Time. By the time the preacher moves to develop a sermon focus and imagery for Advent 2 (and the other Sundays in Advent and Christmas), later in Ordinary Time, she has chosen texts for the Season after Epiphany. During the week that the sermon for Advent 2 is completed by itself, the preacher also spends time interpreting the texts chosen for the season after Epiphany.

Overlapping Tasks

The second process for extending sermon preparation over time involves maintaining a weekly pattern in which an element of preaching preparation takes place each working day. In this model, each day of the work week is consistently given to the same sermon-preparation task, but instead of beginning a sermon on Monday and ending with it on Sunday, the preacher divides up the individual tasks so that every week he is working on three different sermons, and over time the preparation work for every sermon overlaps with the preparation work for numerous other sermons, as well. The weekly schedule would be something like this:[12]

- *Monday & Tuesday*: Finish developing the sermon for the coming Sunday
- *Wednesday*: Interpret biblical text for the sermon two Sundays away.
- *Thursday*: Review sermon for the coming Sunday and develop focus and imagery for the sermon one Sunday away.
- *Sunday*: Preach.

Notice that in this proposed weekly schedule I assume that to avoid pastoral burnout, preachers should hold to a basic five-day workweek that includes Sunday and four weekdays. Therefore, the counting of days includes Fridays and Saturdays as days that are not standard workdays. While I think pastors need to take their call to study continually on behalf of the congregation more seriously, I also think that to be more effective in ministry pastors need to be intentional about maintaining a rhythm of Sabbath.

To someone used to preparing one sermon per week, this overlapping process may, at first glance, seem overly complicated and unnecessarily extended. But the description sounds more complex than the process is in practice. Its rhythm is fairly simple if one is patient enough to live with it for a little while and make it one's own. The benefit comes in the manner in which the preparation for different sermons becomes intimately related to the preparation for other sermons while retaining a separate focus on the individual sermon that might get lost in the proposal to group tasks. Table 2 allows us to examine the way this overlapping process works in relation to an individual sermon. For the sake of illustration, we will again concentrate on the sermon for the Second Sunday of Advent; every task related to preparing this particular sermon is italicized in the chart.

1. The first step of preparing the sermon for Advent 2 is *choosing a bib-lical text*. The text for Advent 2 is chosen in mid-Ordinary Time at the same time all of the Advent and Christmas texts are selected.[13] Choosing the texts this early invites preachers to reflect on the connection between preaching in the last part of Ordinary Time and the preaching that will begin a new liturgical year. Indeed, once the Advent and Christmas texts are chosen and the season has been thought of as a whole, preaching in Ordinary Time can begin to foreshadow aspects of Christian "vocabulary" that one expects to offer in Advent and Christmas. After choosing these texts the preacher puts them aside to deal with more immediate tasks of preaching in the Season after Pentecost.[14] Later in the season (during the week following Pentecost 21 as laid out in table 2), when texts are chosen for the Sundays after Epiphany, preachers can review the Advent and Christmas texts to reconsider the choices and frame the task of choosing texts for Epiphany so that they build on the selections for the previous seasons. This means that by the time preachers turn to the task of preparing individual Advent sermons, they have already been thinking about the relation of Ordinary Time sermons to the Advent texts and have a sense of the general direction of preaching in Christmas and the season after Epiphany. Then, as Advent gets underway, the time arrives to choose texts for Lenten sermons, and the potential connection between preaching in Advent and in the liturgical seasons that follow is extended further.

2. The initial work on the sermon for the Second Sunday of Advent begins with *exegesis* on Wednesday (the day of the week always assigned to biblical interpretation) two and a half weeks before the sermon is to be delivered (see the week following Pentecost 22 on table 2). More specifically, the preacher's first critical look at the Advent 2 text comes in the midst of finalizing the sermon for the Reign of Christ and shaping the focus and imagery for Advent 1. The work done on these other sermons will naturally influence what one looks for in the Advent 2 text and what

aspect of God's hide-and-seek presence in the world one looks through the text to discover.

3. The preacher begins to *develop a focus and brainstorm about imagery* for the Advent 2 sermon on Thursday, a week and a half before the sermon is to be delivered. The exegetical work has been allowed to ferment while developing the focus and imagery for Advent 1, reviewing the sermon for Reign of Christ, delivering the sermon on Reign of Christ, finishing the sermon for Advent 1, and beginning exegesis on the text for Advent 3 (see the weeks beginning with Pentecost 22 and Reign of Christ on table 2). By this point, the process of developing the sermon for Advent 2 has touched sermons related to two Sundays before it and one Sunday after, and the focus that the preacher draws from the earlier exegetical work and in response to the current state of the matrix of conversations is made sharper by the relationship to these preceding and following sermons. Similarly, the imagery chosen for Advent 2 will reverberate with the imagery of adjacent sermons.

4. On Monday and Tuesday of the following week, after the sermon for Advent 1 has been delivered, the preacher returns to the Advent 2 process to *finish developing the sermon*. This step includes sharpening the focus and developing imagery further, deciding on the sermonic form, and writing a draft of the sermon manuscript, notes, or whatever (if anything) will be used in the pulpit. Because this step of the Advent 2 sermon preparation occurs the day after the delivery of the Advent 1 sermon, the "writing" of the sermon is influenced more significantly by the response to that previous sermon than if this step occurred later in the week.

5. The preacher *reviews* the Advent 2 sermon two days later on Thursday—the last workday before Sunday—for possible last-minute revisions (see the week beginning on Advent 1 on table 2). On Wednesday, the draft of the Advent 2 sermon was set aside while the preacher looked ahead to Advent 4 in exegesis, and the review is done on the same day that the preacher develops the initial focus and imagery for the Advent 3 sermon. The ideas developed for the next two weeks may suggest modifications in the Advent 2 sermon to better pave the way for what is coming. In addition, since this editing step is the last task of preaching preparation for the week, the time can also be used to rehearse for Sunday.

6. Finally, on the following Sunday, the preacher steps into the pulpit to *preach* the Second Sunday of Advent sermon. And although this sermon is an individual contribution to the congregation's conversational proclamation with a beginning, middle, and an end, the integrated preaching process has ensured that it will fit well with the sermons that precede and

		TABLE 2		
Sunday	**Monday**	**Tuesday**	**Wednesday**	**Thursday**
Pentecost 16	*Choose Texts for Advent-Christmas*			
	Finish developing sermon for Pent. 17		Exegesis for Pent. 19	Review Pent. 17 / Develop focus/imagery for Pent. 18
Pentecost 17	Finish developing sermon for Pent. 18		Exegesis for Pent. 20	Review Pent. 18 / Develop focus/imagery for Pent. 19
Pentecost 18	Finish developing sermon for Pent. 19		Exegesis for Pent. 21	Review Pent. 19 / Develop focus/imagery for Pent. 20
Pentecost 19	Finish developing sermon for Pent. 20		Exegesis for Pent. 22	Review Pent. 20 / Develop focus/imagery for Pent. 21
Pentecost 20	Finish developing sermon for Pent. 21		Exegesis for Reign of Christ	Review Pent. 21 / Develop focus/imagery for Pent. 22
Pentecost 21	Choose Texts for Epiphany			
	Finish developing sermon for Pent. 22		Exegesis for Advent 1	Review Pent. 22 / Develop focus/imagery for Reign of Christ
Pentecost 22	Finish developing sermon for Reign of Christ		*Exegesis for Advent 2*	Review Reign of Christ / Develop focus/imagery for Advent 1
Reign of Christ	Finish developing sermon for Advent 1		Exegesis for Advent 3	Review Advent 1 / *Develop focus/imagery for Advent 2*
Advent 1	*Finish developing sermon for Advent 2*		Exegesis for Advent 4	*Review Advent 2* / Develop focus/imagery for Advent 3
Advent 2	Finish developing sermon for Advent 3		Exegesis for Xmas 1	Review Advent 3 / Develop focus/imagery for Advent 4
Advent 3	Finish developing sermon for Advent 4		Exegesis for Epiphany	Review Advent 4 / Develop focus/imagery for Xmas 1
Advent 4	Finish developing sermon for Xmas 1		Exegesis for Baptism	Review Xmas 1 / Develop focus/imagery for Epiphany
Xmas 1	Finish developing sermon for Epiphany		Exegesis for Epiphany 2	Review Epiphany / Develop focus/imagery for Baptism
Epiphany	Choose Texts for Lent			
	Finish developing sermon for Baptism		Exegesis for Epiphany 3	Review Baptism / Develop focus/imagery for Epiphany 2
Baptism of Lord	Finish developing sermon for Epiphany 2		Exegesis for Epiphany 4	Review Epiphany 2 / Develop focus/imagery for Epiphany 3
Epiphany 2	Finish developing sermon for Epiphany 3		Exegesis for Epiphany 5	Review Epiphany 3 / Develop focus/imagery for Epiphany 4
Epiphany 3	Finish developing sermon for Epiphany 4		Exegesis for Epiphany 6	Review Epiphany 4 / Develop focus/imagery for Epiphany 5
Epiphany 4	Finish developing sermon for Epiphany 5		Exegesis for Transfiguration	Review Epiphany 5 / Develop focus/imagery for Epiphany 6

TABLE 2 (CONT.)

Sunday	Monday Tuesday	Wednesday	Thursday
Epiphany 5	Finish developing sermon for Epiphany 6	Exegesis for Lent 1	Review Epiphany 6
			Develop focus/imagery for Transfiguration
Epiphany 6	*Choose Texts for Easter*		
	Finish developing sermon for Transfiguration	Exegesis for Lent 2	Review Transfiguration
			Develop focus/imagery for Lent 1
Transfiguration	Finish developing sermon for Lent 1	Exegesis for Lent 3	Review Lent 1
			Develop focus/imagery for Lent 2
Lent 1	Finish developing sermon for Lent 2	Exegesis for Lent 4	Review Lent 2
			Develop focus/imagery for Lent 3
Lent 2	Finish developing sermon for Lent 3	Exegesis for Lent 5	Review Lent 3
			Develop focus/imagery for Lent 4
Lent 3	Finish developing sermon for Lent 4	Exegesis for Palm/ Passion	Review Lent 4
			Develop focus/imagery for Lent 5
Lent 4	Finish developing sermon for Lent 5	Exegesis for Easter Sun.	Review Lent 5
			Develop focus/imagery for Palm/Passion
Lent 5	*Choose Texts for early Ordinary Time*		
	Finish developing sermon for Palm/Passion	Exegesis for Easter 2	Review Palm/Passion
			Develop focus/imagery for Easter Sun.
Palm/Passion	Finish developing sermon for Easter Sun.	Exegesis for Easter 3	Review Easter Sun.
			Develop focus/imagery for Easter 2
Easter Sunday	Finish developing sermon for Easter 2	Exegesis for Easter 4	Review Easter 2
			Develop focus/imagery for Easter 3
Easter 2	Finish developing sermon for Easter 3	Exegesis for Easter 5	Review Easter 3
			Develop focus/imagery for Easter 4
Easter 3	Finish developing sermon for Easter 4	Exegesis for Easter 6	Review Easter 4
			Develop focus/imagery for Easter 5
Easter 4	Finish developing sermon for Easter 5	Exegesis for Ascension	Review Easter 5
			Develop focus/imagery for Easter 6
Easter 5	Finish developing sermon for Easter 6	Exegesis for Pentecost	Review Easter 6
			Develop focus/imagery for Ascension
Easter 6	Finish developing sermon for Ascension	Exegesis for Trinity	Review Ascension
			Develop focus/imagery for Pentecost
Ascension	Finish developing sermon for Pentecost	Exegesis for Pentecost 2	Review Pentecost
			Develop focus/imagery for Trinity
Pentecost	Finish developing sermon for Trinity	Exegesis for Pentecost 3	Review Trinity
			Develop focus/imagery for Pent. 2

follow. There will be a higher level of continuity and progression to the individual snapshots and offerings of "vocabulary" that feeds from the pulpit into the congregation's matrix conversations making meaning of God, self, and the world.

Having sketched two possible processes for connecting different sermons into a unified preaching-preparation process—grouping and overlapping tasks—in part 2 I explore the overlapping process in depth in order to demonstrate that what might sound somewhat complex in description is fairly straightforward in practice. I broaden the focus and discuss preparing all four sermons for Advent, illustrating in detail how this cumulative approach to preaching can contribute to a congregation's ongoing matrix of proclamatory conversations.

Part 2

A Case Study

Chapter 5

A Case Study of
a Conversational Homiletic

When children plead with their parents to stop preaching at them, it is a request for less monologue, more dialogue, fewer clichés, more conversation. Don't the grown-ups in the pews deserve as much . . .

—Robin R. Meyers[1]

I n part 1 of this book, I presented a homiletic in which the church is a community of theological discourse, a matrix of overlapping conversations in which all conversation partners are equally invited (and indeed called) to proclaim their experience of God's presence in the world as part of a process of mutual conversion (i.e., meaning making) that is appropriate to the milieu of cultural postmodernism. What makes these conversations particularly Christian is the commitment to use Christian language in naming, describing, and interpreting God's presence in life and in the world.

In this understanding of the community's possession of and responsibility for proclamation, preaching is not the center of the conversation but one contribution among many to the conversation. Since God is omnipresent, the preacher has no more of an inside track into God's presence than anyone else in the congregation. The preacher does, however, have a unique role in this matrix of conversation as a specialist in the sources of Christian "vocabulary"—Christian Scripture and traditions. When preachers stand in the pulpit on Sunday mornings to offer their snapshot of God's presence as a contribution to the ongoing conversations of the church, they do so with the intent also of resourcing the conversations by offering the traditional "vocabulary" of the Christian faith to be assimilated, used, critiqued, and adapted by all those participating in the community's theological conversations. This view of the preaching office requires a shift in emphasis from the individual sermon as a unique pro-clamatory event to the cumulative contributions of the pastor-preacher to the give-and-take proclamation of the whole community.

In chapter 4 we explored the practical implications of such a cumula-tive approach to preaching. The tension between the call for sermons to work together over time to effect the assimilation of Christian "vocabu-lary" and the need for the individual sermon to be appropriate to the con-versation at that moment resulted in a method of preaching preparation in which the steps of sermon preparation overlap with the preparation of numerous other sermons. In part 2 I explore further the strengths of this homiletical proposal and demonstrate how the process works by detailing the preparation process of four Advent sermons offered to a particular conversational congregation.

The Community of Discourse

My goal in presenting this case study is to examine conversational ser-mons, not to present an exhaustive congregational study. Nevertheless, because conversational sermons are contributions to specific matrixes of conversations, I must briefly describe the congregation for which the ser-mons that follow are intended. The church presented here—that is, its conversations and its struggles—is a composite of congregations I have served in a pastoral role.

Second Downtown Mainline Church has a membership of about 310; active members (those who participate in and support church activities at least somewhat regularly) number about 170; and average worship atten-dance (which includes visitors) is around 130. A downtown congregation in a city of approximately seven hundred thousand, Second Church has had to deal with the effects of urban sprawl. As suburbanization and white flight increased in the 1960s and 1970s, membership decreased. Salaries, utilities, building maintenance, and programs were becoming a financial burden that the shrinking congregation could not carry.

Instead of looking inward or backward, however, at this point the church retooled itself and began to look forward, focusing on a ministry reaching out to the inner-city population and especially addressing issues related to urban poverty. A variety of food, shelter, clothing, and coun-seling services was established. The result was successful in that many inner-city residents received essential services from the church. However, these people primarily remained in a client relationship with the church;

few of them actually joined the church and began sharing in the congregational ministry. Instead, as the church emphasized peace and justice ministries, moderate and liberal middle-class Christians who had an interest in social concerns began to drive into the city from the suburbs to be a part of the congregation and participate in its work. Thus a congregation with a vital ministry grew, but barely enough to meet rising expenses. After three decades of being a congregation in service to, but in important ways disconnected from, the community in which it resides, Second Church needed to revision its mission once again.

Since there was no crisis facing the church as there had been in the early 1970s, this revisioning could be slower and more deliberate. And, indeed, the spark that got the conversation about the future going was a gift of $180,000 left to the church in a will of a member who had long since moved away. Formal and informal discussions arose concerning how the money should be used. Many ideas were proposed, but most fell into two categories: 1) extending the social justice ministries of the church and 2) dealing with the deferred maintenance needs of the building. The speed with which this debate became divisive led the leaders of the church to lay aside for a year the issue of how to use the money and instead plan a series of conversations concerning the future of Second Church that would inform this and other important decisions.

The initial phase of the series of conversations was to be comprised of small group sessions held in members' homes. The conversations would follow a plan: First, the older members who were around before and through the retooling were to share their memories of the church. Next, small group conversations would be established for all members to share memories and celebrations about the church in the time that they have been a member. Then small groups would identify and discuss areas where the ministries of the congregation needed attention and improvement. All of these conversations would inform small groups focused on the direction the church needed to take in the near and distant future. Plenty of time would be allowed for tangents to be followed in all of these levels of conversation. In a late phase of the series, these small group conversations would feed into larger and larger conversations until some level of consensus was achieved so that a congregational decision could be made about specific plans for the future. At that point, it would be clearer how the $180,000 gift and other resources of the congregation should best be used.

These conversations were to be spread out over the course of a year and would begin in mid-October. Of course, while they would dominate much of Second Church's conversational energy and would be the primary conversations to involve the entire congregation, they were not the only conversation circles active in the congregation:

- Both the monthly men's group and the monthly women's group are (independently) in the midst of a process of sharing autobiographies. The groups gather for a meal and then a person who has volunteered spends 20–30 minutes telling her or his life story in whatever way she or he wishes. Afterwards, others gathered engage the presenter in conversation until the meeting is closed with a prayer offered in thanks for the presenter's life.
- A weekly Wednesday morning Bible study composed of older women is completing a study of the Psalms and will be starting a study that looks at women in the Bible.
- The older adult Sunday school class follows the International Sunday School Lesson plan as it has for forty years. These lessons are grouped together around themes and biblical texts. In the fall, the biblical texts are drawn from shorter, non-Pauline epistles and in December the theme focuses on the incarnation.
- A second adult Sunday school class focuses on spirituality. During the last quarter of the year, they are discussing the discipline of prayer.
- A third adult class prefers a variety of studies that begin and end in a fairly short span of time. People come and go from the class depending on the topic, but the core group is constant. And since they choose topics and approaches that vary, they often invite guest teachers to lead them in their discussions. During the fall they are discussing peace-related issues, such as just war theory, nuclear disarmament, current situations of political violence, etc. In November of each year, this group invites the pastor to give a three-week overview of the Gospel that is the primary focus of the coming lectionary year. Following this overview, they spend a couple of months studying the Gospel. The lectionary cycle to begin in Advent will be Year C, so the Gospel to be discussed is Luke.
- The youth Sunday school class uses a lectionary-based curriculum.
- The youth group that meets on Sunday evenings has asked the youth minister to lead a study on the Apostles' Creed. This will begin in November, so the group will be discussing issues related to the virgin birth and the nature of Jesus as Advent rolls around.
- The children's Sunday school class uses denominational curriculum that is biblically based but timed to fit loosely with the liturgical

year. When Advent rolls around, the class will be focusing on the story of Jesus' birth.

With this general introduction to Second Church and with some of its proclamatory conversations before us, we turn to the process of preparing and delivering sermons for Second Church's celebration of the season of Advent. I have chosen Advent not for some special significance of this liturgical season, but simply because the four-week period offers a manageable number of sermons to deal with in this case study.

MONDAY, OCTOBER 6
Choosing Biblical Texts for Advent 1–4[2]

Second Church uses the Revised Common Lectionary (RCL) in worship, straying from it rarely and only when the lectionary choices do not flow well week-to-week, or when there are special occasions or particular congregational needs. In Ordinary Time, preceding the season of Advent, we had chosen to use the continuous readings offered by the RCL. It was Year B of the three-year cycle, and through most of the season after Pentecost, sermons had focused on the Gospel of Mark. During the last couple of months of Ordinary Time in Year B of the lectionary cycle, we shifted sermonic attention to the readings from Hebrews. While preaching through Hebrews (two months before the beginning of Advent), the time to choose texts for Advent of Year C arrived.

Although sermons are my particular responsibility and my most significant contribution to the congregational conversations, the director of Christian education, music minister, and I perform the task of choosing texts together. We have weekly staff meetings in which we take care of a variety of regular tasks, one of which is keeping each other informed about the matrix of conversations since we participate in different conversation circles throughout the congregation. This discussion informs occasional tasks, such as choosing texts to focus the whole of worship and, especially, the sermon.

As the three of us gathered for our staff meeting in early October to consider texts for Advent, we discussed the general state of conversations then going on throughout the congregation and identified congregational conversations anticipated for around the time of Advent that should influence our choices of texts. At the top of the list, of course, were the conversations concerning the future of the church. The director of Christian education mentioned that some children and youth conversations would focus on Advent and Christmas themes and one adult Sunday school class would begin studying Luke at the beginning of the new lectionary cycle. This talk of Advent's scheduled conversations also reminded the music minister of a regular but unplanned conversation that occurs in and beyond the choir every Advent—it is a discussion that usually begins with someone arguing that once Thanksgiving has passed, Christmas carols should be sung in worship. With this broad sense of where the congregation's conversations were heading, the three of us turned to the task of choosing texts for the Advent sermons. We were not simply looking for individual texts to be used in individual worship services, but for texts that invite a cumulative approach to preaching.

We had each glanced at the lectionary before we gathered. As I did so, I quickly (and imprecisely) labeled the different texts both to help me remember what I had read when we discussed the texts and to get an initial sense of connections among the texts and of progression across the four Sundays:

Sunday	RCL	Theme
Advent 1	Jeremiah 33:14–16	Righteous Branch from David
	Psalm 25:1–10	Prayer for guidance
	1 Thessalonians 3:9–13	Paul's blessing of the Thessalonian church
	Luke 21:25–36	Eschatological discourse
Advent 2	Malachi 3:1–4	Messenger of the coming of the Lord
	Luke 1:68–79	Benedictus
	Philippians 1:3-11	Opening prayer for the Philippian church
	Luke 3:1–6	Description of John the Baptist (Isaiah quote)
Advent 3	Zephaniah 3:14–20	Vision of the Day of the Lord—Rejoice!
	Isaiah 12:2–6	Song of praise for God's salvation
	Philippians 4:4–7	Rejoice in the Lord always!
	Luke 3:7–18	John the Baptist's preaching
Advent 4	Micah 5:2–5a	Ruler shall come from Bethlehem
	Luke 1:46b–55	Magnificat
	Hebrews 10:5–10	Christ's sacrifice ("When Christ came into the World")
	Luke 1:39–45	Mary and Elizabeth

We initially considered focusing on the Gospel lections for all four Sundays to allow worship to continue with some sense of *lectio continua* while engaging the conversation circle studying Luke and introducing the Gospel for the year to the whole congregation right off the bat. But we soon agreed on two more important goals: helping the congregation better assimilate the "vocabulary" of Advent and engaging the central conversation of revisioning Second Church. This led us to decide to emphasize the eschatological character of the season, especially since eschatology is a part of Christian "vocabulary" that has been lost in mainline congregations.

This decision focused our attention on the prophetic texts from the Hebrew Bible readings. Preaching on these texts, which present visions of God's future, offered the potential to make a significant contribution to the conversation about the congregation's future. After preaching through much of Mark and Hebrews during Ordinary Time, the turn to the Hebrew Bible seemed a good expansion of biblical "vocabulary" as well, and the turn to the Prophets would also allow me to challenge some interpretations of ancient prophecy as fortune-telling-type predictions related either to Jesus or to our day.

Just as we were about to close our conversation, the music minister suggested that on the Fourth Sunday of Advent we focus on the Lukan texts (the Gospel reading and the Magnificat, which the RCL substitutes for a reading from the Psalter) instead of Micah 5:2–5a. She viewed the Magnificat as a prophetic oracle and argued that by reading this passage in a series of prophetic texts, a woman would be lifted up as a prophet and the eschatological character of Christ's birth and Christmas (as opposed to the idea that eschatology leads up to Jesus and not beyond) would be introduced. The director of Christian education supported the idea and noted that this presentation of Mary would engage the Bible study group looking at women in the Bible. So we all agreed that the texts for Advent sermons would be as follows:

Advent 1	Jeremiah 33:14–16	Righteous Branch from David
Advent 2	Malachi 3:1–4	Messenger of the coming of the Lord
Advent 3	Zephaniah 3:14–20	Vision of the Day of the Lord— Rejoice!
Advent 4	Luke 1:39–56	Mary and Elizabeth and the Magnificat

I laid these texts aside for a while as I continued preaching through Hebrews. By the time I would begin exegesis on the text for the First Sunday of Advent,

TABLE 3				
Sunday	**Monday/Tuesday**	**Wednesday**	**Thursday**	**Friday/Saturday**
Pentecost 21	Choose texts for Epiphany			Days off
(Heb. 9:24–28) 11/09	Finish developing Pent. 22 (Heb. 10:11–18) 11/10–11	Exegesis for Advent 1 (Jer. 33:14–16) 11/12	Review Pent. 22 (Heb. 10:11–18) Develop focus/imagery for Reign of Christ (Heb. 12:1–3) 11/13	 11/14–15
Pentecost 22 (Heb. 10:11-18) 11/16	Finish developing Reign of Christ (Heb. 12:1–3) 11/17–18	Exegesis for Advent 2 (Mal. 3:1-4) 11/19	Review Reign of Christ (Heb. 12:1–3) Develop focus/imagery for Advent 1 (Jer. 33:14–16) 11/20	Days Off 11/21–22
Reign of Christ (Heb. 12:1–3) 11/23	Finish developing Advent 1 (Jer. 33:14–16) 11/24–25	Exegesis for Advent 3 (Zeph. 3:14–20) 11/26	Review Advent 1 (Jer. 33:14–16) Develop focus/imagery for Advent 2 (Mal. 3:1–4) 11/27	Days off 11/28–29
Advent 1 (Jer. 33:14–16) 11/30	Finish developing Advent 2 (Mal. 3:1–4) 12/01–02	Exegesis for Advent 4 (Luke 1:39–56) 12/03	Review Advent 2 (Mal. 3:1–4) Develop focus/imagery for Advent 3 (Zeph. 3:14–20) 12/04	Days off 12/05–06
Advent 2 (Mal. 3:1–4) 12/07	Finish developing Advent 3 (Zeph. 3:14–20) 12/08–09	Exegesis for Xmas 1 (John 1:1–18) 12/10	Review Advent 3 (Zeph. 3:14–20) Develop focus/imagery for Advent 4 (Luke 1:39–56) 12/11	Days off 12/12–13
Advent 3 (Zeph. 3:14–20) 12/14	Finish developing Advent 4 (Luke 1:39–56) 12/15–16	Exegesis for Epiphany (Matt. 2:1–12) 12/17	Review Advent 4 (Luke 1:39–56) Develop focus/imagery for Xmas 1 (John 1:1–18) 12/18	Days off 12/19–20
Advent 4 (Luke 1:39–56) 12/21				

Ordinary Time would be drawing to a close, and we would have chosen texts for the seasons of Christmas and Epiphany.

In working on these sermons, I followed the proposal for overlapping tasks offered on pp. 80–85. To aid in the discussion of preparing these sermons, I have excerpted the portion of table 2 on p. 83 that applies to the preparation and delivery of Advent sermons and inserted specific dates and biblical texts to create table 3.

WEDNESDAY, NOVEMBER 12
Exegesis for Advent 1
About two months after choosing the texts for Advent, I took my first critical, exegetical look at the text assigned for the First Sunday of Advent. On my mind were both the sermon I had just preached the previous Sunday on Heb. 9:24–28 (see Pentecost 21 on Table 3) and the one I had just finished developing on Heb. 10:11–18 on Monday and Tuesday for the coming Sunday (Pentecost 22). Both sermons dealt with soteriology and the biblical author's understanding of the uniqueness of the sacrifice of the cross.

I was also thinking about the congregational conversation concerning the future of the church, now underway. It was still early, but the congregation was taking the process very seriously. Older members had begun to share their memories of earlier days in the church so that many in the church now shared a better appreciation of where we had been as a community of faith. We were now moving into the conversational step where people share their more recent memories and the things they celebrate about the life and ministry of Second Church. Even though we had planned later discussions of strengths and weaknesses, joys and sorrows, many of the celebratory comments already had a "but" tied to them that foreshadowed two themes that would probably become important issues in our year-long conversation. First, while members continued to be strongly committed to the needs of the inner-city residents of the community around the church, some were frustrated because we constantly seemed to be addressing symptoms of injustice and poverty rather than the corrupt systems that create the problems. Second, some members, while expressing their satisfaction with our struggle to meet the needs of victims of inequitable distribution of economic resources, did not always feel that their own spiritual needs were being met.

Also, I reminded myself of the thematic emphases we discussed when we chose the texts for Advent—helping the congregation better assimilate the "vocabulary" of Advent and eschatology.

With these things on my mind, I began my Wednesday morning task of exegesis. I had set aside on my appointment calendar two and a half hours each morning for sermon preparation. I often do not use all of the time, and at times I need more, but I keep this time slot blocked on my calendar and allow nothing but emergencies to encroach upon it.

As I began exegesis, I looked for ways the text could help me contribute to the congregation's task of interpreting our mission in the world as the body of Christ located in our particular inner-city setting, and for the ways this text could help me focus a vision of God's presence in this situation. Since I work on more than one sermon at a time, I use a different legal pad for making notes for each individual sermon to keep my work organized. Thus, I begin with a clean legal pad and make notes using my standard exegetical process. After reading through the text aloud several times, I jot down first impressions and initial questions concerning the text. I explore the passage's historical and literary contexts. I attend to rhetorical structure and flow, especially noticing if and how the passage climaxes. And I struggle with what types of theological and social issues are raised in the text.

So I began this morning's session by reading aloud a couple of times Jer. 33:14–16, the lection we chose for Advent 1:

> [14] The days are surely coming, says the LORD, when I will fulfill the promise I made to the house of Israel and the house of Judah. [15] In those days and at that time I will cause a righteous Branch to spring up for David; and he shall execute justice and righteousness in the land. [16] In those days Judah will be saved and Jerusalem will live in safety. And this is the name by which it shall be called: 'The LORD is our righteousness.'

And then I jotted down a number of first impressions and questions:

> The text is thoroughly eschatological, as indicated by the four references to "the days" to come.
>
> The tone of the oracle seems to indicate reversal—presumably there is not justice and righteousness in the land at the time the oracle is pronounced. Does this tone (along with the specific reference to Jerusalem) mean this oracle comes from the exilic period?
>
> This reversal theme is related to the promise to restore the Davidic line, which is why the early church and the RCL traditionally relate the text to the coming of Christ. How do I preach this text without the congregation hearing "Jesus" for "Branch of David" whether I want them to or not?
>
> The justice language of the passage fits well with the theological leanings of Second Church. What does it mean to think eschatologically about justice in the city as the congregation struggles with social ministries that seem only to scratch the surface and not deal with the causes of injustice?
>
> These three verses feel plucked out of their context. Has the RCL divided the text improperly (as it often does)?

This last observation led me into the literary context of the lection. As I began to explore the wider context, I found a note in my study Bible that 33:14–26 must be a later addition to Jeremiah, since these verses do not appear in the Septuagint. And, indeed, the way they are inserted makes them part of the oracle beginning at 33:1 where the setting is established: "The word of the LORD came to Jeremiah a second time, while he was still confined in the court of the guard. . . ." Thus the complete passage is 33:1–26. While the RCL's division of the text is too short, twenty-six verses are too long to read in worship. Perhaps further study would offer a different delineation of a passage to be read and preached on.

The "second time" (33:1) refers back to the "first time" the word of the Lord came to Jeremiah—during the siege of Jerusalem described in 32:1–15. Although Jeremiah is presented as prophesying God's judgment prior to the siege, during a time of overly optimistic prosperity (32:3–5), he offers a very different message once God's judgment and horrifying suffering have arrived. In this first oracle from prison, God instructs Jeremiah to purchase a field from his cousin as a sign that houses and fields and vineyards would be bought once again in Judah.

The "second time" of chapter 33 is an oracle from the court of the guard that has the same tone of hope in the midst of great distress as the first time the Lord's word came to Jeremiah. It opens with a graphic description of the destruction in Jerusalem wrought by the invasion of the Babylonians (33:4–6) but then shifts dramatically to a promise of restoration (v. 7). This restoration will include the cleansing of guilt (v. 8), sounds of joy related to weddings and sacrificial offerings (vv. 10–11), replenishing of flocks (vv. 12–13), a just ruler from the line of David (vv. 14–16), and the reaffirmation of the Davidic and Levitical covenants (vv. 19–26). The way this structure is laid out, an obvious place to break in the passage is at verse 16. Therefore, the reading I will use in worship is 33:1–16.

As I studied the oracle as a whole I am struck by the view of salvation as not some pie-in-the-sky rescue by a *deus ex machina* but an eschatological vision of a return to normalcy—a time after war and exile when land is bought and sold, sons and daughters are given away in marriage, people sing traditional hymns while making offerings at the temple, and flocks graze in pastures. What further struck me is the inclusion of a ruler who will execute justice and righteousness as part of the view of what should be (at least eschatologically speaking) the normal state of affairs.

Having spent my morning thinking about this text, I lay my exegetical notes aside to ferment until I return to them in eight days.

THURSDAY, NOVEMBER 13
Review for Pentecost 22

Develop Focus & Imagery for Reign of Christ
Today, I first reviewed and rehearsed my sermon on Heb. 10:11–18 for the coming Sunday. In it I deal with the writer's understanding of the unique nature of Christ's sacrifice.

Then I returned to my exegetical notes on Heb. 12:1–3 and began developing a focus and imagery with which to offer that focus to the congregation on the following Sunday (Reign of Christ). We had decided to break from the RCL's options for the Reign of Christ, the last Sunday in Ordinary Time, in order to continue reading in Hebrews for one more week. This short passage was chosen, however, because of its reference to the enthronement of Jesus at the right hand of God. My sermon will explore the modern christological significance of the ancient claims about Christ's exaltation.

FRIDAY–SATURDAY, NOVEMBER 14–15
Days Off

SUNDAY, NOVEMBER 16
Preach on Pentecost 22
I preached my sermon on Heb. 10:11–18.

MONDAY–TUESDAY, NOVEMBER 17–18
Finish Developing Sermon for Reign of Christ
Building on the exegetical work begun twelve days prior and my initial brainstorming about a sermonic focus and imagery (from four days prior), I spent two mornings "writing" my sermon on Heb. 12:1–3 for the coming Sunday.

WEDNESDAY, NOVEMBER 19
Exegesis for Advent 2
Having completed my sermon for this Sunday, I now turned to the task of interpreting Mal. 3:1–4 for the Second Sunday of Advent. As I did, I had on my mind Sunday's sermon on Hebrews 12 as well as the exegetical work I did on Jeremiah 33 for Advent 1. As always I began by reading the text aloud several times:

> 3:1See, I am sending my messenger to prepare the way before me, and the Lord whom you seek will suddenly come to his temple. The mes-

senger of the covenant in whom you delight—indeed, he is coming, says the LORD of hosts. [2] But who can endure the day of his coming, and who can stand when he appears?

For he is like a refiner's fire and like fullers' soap; [3] he will sit as a refiner and purifier of silver, and he will purify the descendants of Levi and refine them like gold and silver, until they present offerings to the LORD in righteousness. [4] Then the offering of Judah and Jerusalem will be pleasing to the LORD as in days of old and as in former years.

I pulled out a fresh legal pad and jotted down initial impressions and questions. For example,

> The RCL has subordinated the original intention behind this text to the gospel reading, which relates to John the Baptist (Luke 3:1–6). What is the original historical and theological context of the oracle?
> The passage is thoroughly eschatological. The language of "coming" of the Lord fits with Advent.
> Who is "the messenger of the covenant"? Are the messenger and the Lord of v. 1 the same? Why is Lord in v. 1 not written in small caps as in vv. 3 and 4 (presumably this "Lord" is not a translation of "Yahweh")?
> Is it the messenger or God who brings judgment and refining?
> As with the Jeremiah text for Advent 1, this passage looks like it has been truncated to fit its liturgical use.
> The references to silver and gold remind me of the Burl Ives' song "Silver and Gold" in the children's holiday special "Rudolf the Rednosed Reindeer."
> The tone of judgment in vv. 1–3a lead to the hope of faithfulness in v. 3b–4.
> The reference to the temple gives the impression that Malachi is not an exilic prophet. Indeed this passage seems to be a critique of temple practice and temple leadership/priesthood. How will the temple reformation imagery be heard (and how would I like it to be heard) by the congregation while we are reexamining the vision of Second Church?

My initial glance at the passage made it clear that I needed an overview of Malachi. Since only this passage and 4:1–2a (Proper 28, Year C) appear in the RCL from Malachi, I have not preached from Malachi much and am in need of some sense of the context in which it was produced. I turned quickly to general introductions to the book as a whole before diving deeper into the passage. The Hebrew name *Malachi* means "my messenger." Nothing outside of the reference in this book is known of a historical prophet named Malachi, so it is unclear whether "Malachi" is an actual person or a symbolic name. The criticism of temple practice indicates that the book was written after the second temple had been built and rededicated. Indeed, the introduction to Malachi in my study Bible states that the overall message of the book is that God is displeased with the lack of piety in the community gathered around the temple and is sending a messenger to purify it.

There are six oracles in the book, and each follows a basic pattern of an opening affirmation in the form of a question or statement, a response that calls the affirmation into question, and an explication or amplification that reaffirms the opening. The lection for Advent 2 is part of the fourth oracle, which extends from 2:17 to 3:5. The whole passage would be structured as follows:

Opening affirmation: 2:17You have wearied the LORD with your words.

Response: Yet you say, "How have we wearied him?"

Amplification: By saying, "All who do evil are good in the sight of the LORD, and he delights in them." Or by asking, "Where is the God of justice?"

3:1See, I am sending my messenger to prepare the way before me, and the Lord whom you seek will suddenly come to his temple. The messenger of the covenant in whom you delight—indeed, he is coming, says the LORD of hosts. 2 But who can endure the day of his coming, and who can stand when he appears?

For he is like a refiner's fire and like fullers' soap; 3 he will sit as a refiner and purifier of silver, and he will purify the descendants of Levi and refine them like gold and silver, until they present offerings to the LORD in righteousness. 4 Then the offering of Judah and Jerusalem will be pleasing to the LORD as in days of old and as in former years.

5 Then I will draw near to you for judgment; I will be swift to bear witness against the sorcerers, against the adulterers, against those who swear falsely, against those who oppress the hired workers, the widow and the orphan, against those

who thrust aside the alien, and do not fear me, says the LORD of hosts.

The Advent 2 lection has a very different tone when it is read as part of the full oracle instead of in isolation and in reference to John the Baptist. The focus of the oracle is neither the temple nor the messenger. Rather, the focus is on God's offering an eschatological response to the question of theodicy: why do those who do evil seem blessed and why does God not come to bring justice? The answer is that God is *coming* to judge and refine. The corruption in temple practice is one symptom among others with which God will deal; the others include sorcery; adultery; perjury; oppression of laborers, widows, and orphans; and xenophobia. The use of "then" in verse 5, moreover, implies that God will deal with temple practice first before dealing with social injustices. In other words, from the viewpoint of the prophet, social injustice flows out of religious impiety, and the establishment of proper religious practice leads to social reform. This recognition led me to decide to have the full oracle (2:17–3:5) read in worship and to base my sermon on the longer reading.

When I turned to commentaries to explore the oracle in more depth and test my initial observations, I found a couple of things of interest:

> Many scholars argue that the shift from first person and second person in 2:17–3:1a to third person in 3:1b–4 and back to first person in 3:5 signals that the original oracle was 2:17–3:1a, 5 and the material in the middle was developed and added later.
>
> Scholars are just as confused as I about the identity in 3:1 of "my messenger," the "Lord [as opposed to LORD] whom you seek," and the "messenger of the covenant" (a phrase that only appears here in the Old Testament). Some argue that they are all one in the same— Yahweh. Some think the messenger refers to the prophet "Malachi" himself but this would seem to diminish the eschatological nature of the passage. Others connect this messenger language with 4:5—"Lo, I will send you the prophet Elijah before the great and terrible day of the LORD comes." In the end, however, the emphasis is not on the identity to which these labels point but the refining results of his/their coming.
>
> In v. 5 participles are used in describing the acts to be condemned. The verb form suggests habitual conduct and attitudes.

At the end of my time devoted to exegesis, I was drawn toward exploring the way in which the text views the functioning of the temple as intimately related to social concerns. In the context of contemporary Christianity and especially Second Church's conversation about its struggle to be in social ministry, I was interested in struggling in my sermon with the relation of inner church practice to issues of social justice. How does a contemporary reflection on eschatology offer guidance for this struggle?

THURSDAY, NOVEMBER 20
Review for Reign of Christ

Develop Focus & Imagery for Advent 1

Today I reviewed and rehearsed my sermon for the Reign of Christ. Then, I moved to the task of developing the primary focus for the sermon for Advent 1. I now had to 1) determine how Jer. 33:1–16 focuses our view of God's presence in the world and 2) reflect on the elements of Christian "vocabulary" that this text invites me to offer to the congregation on the particular occasion of the First Sunday of Advent. I also needed to think about the kinds of contributions I wanted to make to the ongoing matrix of conversations throughout the congregation.

To begin, I reread Jer. 33:1–16 aloud; then I reviewed my earlier exegetical notes on the text in light of the sermons I have preached and prepared recently and in light of the conversations in the church. A couple of thoughts grabbed my attention and would not let go. First, using the texts in Hebrews, my sermons in late Ordinary Time had focused on individualistic, existential approaches to salvation, but Jeremiah speaks of salvation in communal, social terms. Following immediately the sermons on Hebrews, this sermon would allow me to expand the "vocabulary" of salvation that is most familiar to most in the church. Second, I felt a strong connection with those who have expressed frustration over the fact that while the church did much to meet the immediate needs of those on the margins of society, we did little in terms of changing those broader societal structures that marginalize.

These two issues were clearly related, and I chose to develop a sermonic focus that would deal with both: *The salvation for which we hope and toward which we work is not simply some pie-in-the-sky salvation for me, but instead is the establishment of social, economic, and political normalcy for all.* This focus draws on the eschatological and social orientation of the biblical text and is expressed in terms of contrast between what I wanted to suggest salvation is not and what I wanted to suggest it is, which might serve to establish a basic sermonic form.

I wrote this focus statement at the top of a new page in my notepad and began brainstorming ideas, language, and imagery for the sermon. At this point, anything that comes to mind gets jotted down, for I do not want to stifle my creativity by putting limits on or organizing my thoughts; filtering and structuring come at a later stage. Some ideas flowed quickly, and others, more slowly. Here's what I wrote:

Stereotypical views of salvation: getting to heaven with streets of gold, pearly gates, etc.; free from all worries; Utopia.

Don't forget this is Advent 1: should I use sermon time to reintroduce the "vocabulary" of Advent, liturgical year, etc.?

Salvific experiences that are not extraordinary but return to normalcy (for analogies): remission from cancer; getting out of serious debt; getting out of an abusive relationship; starting to date again after divorce; getting back into a daily routine after something throws life into a tailspin; after depression—not happy, but normal array of emotions; forgiveness (making-up) after an argument; rebuilding after tornado; returning to work after layoff/strike.

Weekly volunteer experience in a homeless shelter I had some years ago—same people week after week; no one ever seemed to escape.

Second Church is located across street from City Hall—religion and politics on opposite side of the same street, hmm? How can they meet in the street?

City has recently passed a new vagrancy law restricting homeless people from loitering in public parks.

In a recent small group meeting, Karen said, "I am really proud of our soup kitchen ministry, but then I hear someone say, 'If you give someone a fish you feed them for a day; if you teach them to fish, you feed them for a lifetime,' and I feel less pleased. But then it gets worse when I think, yeah we could teach them to fish but will anyone let them near the lake?"

Advent means to "come to": in this season we focus not only on getting ready for Christmas (the celebration of God coming to us in the birth of Jesus) but on the idea that God is *always* coming to us. Still, few people wait at their windows looking for Jesus to come surfing in on the clouds. What does it mean to "expect God to come to us"? (Do people really expect God in the future at all anymore?)

How does the establishment (i.e., restoration) of social and economic normalcy envisioned in Jeremiah relate to the Sunday school discussion next week about Luke's thematic emphases on salvation as reversal and on the sharing of possessions?

Deus ex machina—Ancient Greek plays presented a god of the rafters lowered by a machine who "saves the day" at the last moment of the play and makes everything all right. This is not Jeremiah's vision of salvation.

Christian traditions have used many metaphors/theories to describe salvation: atonement, redemption, ransom, reconciliation, justification, satisfaction, new creation. How do these relate to Jeremiah's societal view of salvation?

Long-term prisoners have a difficult time returning to normalcy as defined outside prison (e.g., *Shawshank Redemption*).

For those on the bottom of the socioeconomic ladder to experience normalcy, there must be a redistribution of resources and opportunities.

How do I deal with social ills and point toward salvific hope instead of creating feelings of hopelessness and guilt?

Marrying—familial life; shepherds—economic life; Davidic ruler—political life. What has to happen for people to have access to all of the arenas of life?

Faith is the assurance of things hoped for . . . (Heb. 11:1).

Modern misconceptions of biblical prophecy—not séance-type predictions, but sociopolitical analysis informed by theology and vice versa. Jeremiah did not have to be a seer to recognize that the Babylonian Empire was going to conquer little Judah any more than an Iraqi would have needed a crystal ball to recognize that the U.S. would conquer Iraq. (How far would I want to go in this sermon with an image such as this that draws an analogy between the U.S. and Babylon as the evil colonizer that was yet asserting God's judgment?)

Kinds of structural issues underlying marginalization of individuals: sexism; ageism; classicism; uneven access to education, healthcare, employment.

In a recent committee meeting on our transition shelter for recovering addicts, someone mentioned that the phone in the shelter is always answered with a simple "Hello," instead of something like "Second Church Shelter." This is done in case a potential employer is calling to secure an interview or offer a job to someone—we don't want to spoil their chances. One of the reasons homeless people often can't get jobs is that they are not able to list permanent phone numbers and addresses on applications. Could we expand our services so people can receive e-mail and phone messages here whether they are living in the shelter or not?

After writing down as many questions, ideas, stories, images and metaphors that came to mind in the amount of time I had set aside after reviewing this Sunday's sermon, I laid aside the focus and brainstorming notes and let them germinate until the beginning of the upcoming work week.

FRIDAY–SATURDAY, NOVEMBER 21–22
Days Off

SUNDAY, NOVEMBER 23
Preach on Reign of Christ
I preach my sermon on Heb. 12:1–3.

MONDAY–TUESDAY, NOVEMBER 24–25
Finish Developing Sermon for Advent 1
I returned now to the sermon material I had developed thus far for the First Sunday of Advent. I began by reminding myself of my focus: *The salvation for which we hope and toward which we work is not some pie-in-the-sky salvation for me, but instead is the establishment of social, economic, and political normalcy for all.* I reread Jer. 33:1–16 aloud, reviewed my exegetical notes, and glanced over my brainstorming notes.

While an individual sermon needs a grounding focus, every sermon does many things. Since this is the First Sunday of Advent, I wanted to use the sermon to introduce the broad theme of Advent-eschatology that would ground all four Sundays of the season. But I wanted to develop a single sermon, not two sermons spoken in the time set for one, and these different elements led me to consider a didactic sermon.

Since the sermonic focus is structured as a contrast and I had already considered a contrasting structure for the sermon, I played for a minute with the idea of structuring the sermon around a series of contrasts:

Pie-in-the-sky salvation	Earthly salvation
Realized salvation	Eschatological salvation
Advent as pre-Christmas	Advent as eschatological
Salvation as individual	Salvation as social
Salvation as something radically new, ecstatic	Salvation as restoration of normalcy
God of the past	God of the future

Pre-1970s Second Church	Post-1970s Second Church
Addressing oppressive symptoms	Addressing oppressive systems
Prophecy as prediction	Prophecy as sociotheological analysis
Jeremiah's preexilic oracles of judgment	Jeremiah's exilic oracles of hope
Traditional use of this passage as referring to Jesus	Place of this oracle in Jeremiah's original historical context
Literal interpretation of eschatology	Metaphorical/symbolic interp. of eschatology
Secular calendar	Liturgical calendar
Secular new year (Advent 1)	Christian new year (Advent)

Could a didactic sermon be structured by a series of contrasts such as these, ordered to lead up to an affirmation of the focus I had chosen? The order might be something like this:

> We live by lots of calendars
>   1. Secular Time
>   Christian Time
>   2. Secular Christmas Season
>   Liturgical Advent Season
> The "End"
>   1. Culture's focus on *Now*
>   Biblical focus on *Then*
>   2. Literal Misinterpretation of End
>   Prophetic Interpretation of End
> An Advent vision of Salvation
>   1. Jeremiah's *Now*
>   Jeremiah's *Then*
>   2. Our *Now*
>   Our hope for *Then*

I liked the feel of these contrasts building into one another, but overall there seemed to be too much of a pendulum feel to the flow and too much material before the sermon began to contrast understandings of salvation. The emphasis in the sermon should, I realized, be on developing and exploring the view of God's presence in the world in terms of establishing normalcy, and this structure would leave little time for that. Instead, I needed to think about the ending of the sermon, and then rework the introductory contrasts to move toward that ending.

I wanted the sermon to end with a concrete image of normalcy being (re)established in a social context as a vision of salvation and of Second Church's mission as it continued its conversation about its future. I hadn't yet come up with that image, but I could still think about the flow of the sermon to get to that point. I knew also that I wanted to begin the sermon with a look at Advent in general as part of my regular teaching about our church practices. I also wanted to engage both the youth who were turning to Advent themes in their Sunday school conversations and those who would be discussing issues related to Advent and Christmas music in worship. So my sermon needed to flow from a broad look at Advent to a narrow view of salvation as the establishment of normalcy. I come up with this order:

> Advent as eschatological envisioning of God's coming
> Jeremiah's eschatological vision of salvation as social, economic, and
>   political normalcy
> A vision of Second Church's role in establishing normalcy

The first two movements could still be characterized by contrasts although they worked in a more easily flowing, less pendulum-like manner. I began to work on language for different parts of the sermon, filtering through some of the imagery I had already thought about and developing some new imagery. At this point I still didn't know the specific image with which I would end, but I did know how I wanted the image to function. As I began crafting earlier parts of the sermon, an image came to mind that could serve as the ending. It was an occasion of the church hosting a Christmas Day party for families in a shelter. At the end of the party a woman thanked us for helping her feel normal. It was not as powerful an image as I hoped to find, but as a shared memory of many in the congregation it will work well at the close of the sermon.

When my two mornings' work was done, I had a solid draft of a sermon manuscript prepared.

WEDNESDAY, NOVEMBER 26
Exegesis for Advent 3

With Sunday's sermon on Jeremiah 33 fresh in my mind and my exegetical work on Mal. 2:17–3:5 in the back of my mind, I turned to the text for the Third Sunday of Advent: Zeph. 3:14–20. I pulled out a blank legal pad so I could make notes, and I began reading through the text aloud several times:

3:14 Sing aloud, O daughter Zion;
      shout, O Israel!
    Rejoice and exult with all your heart,
      O daughter Jerusalem!
15 The LORD has taken away the judgments against you,
      he has turned away your enemies.
    The king of Israel, the LORD, is in your midst;
      you shall fear disaster no more.
16 On that day it shall be said to Jerusalem:
    Do not fear, O Zion;
      do not let your hands grow weak.
17 The LORD, your God, is in your midst,
      a warrior who gives victory;
    he will rejoice over you with gladness,
      he will renew you in his love;
    he will exult over you with loud singing
18   as on a day of festival.
    I will remove disaster from you,
      so that you will not bear reproach for it.
19 I will deal with all your oppressors
      at that time.
    And I will save the lame
      and gather the outcast,
    and I will change their shame into praise
      and renown in all the earth.
20 At that time I will bring you home,
      at the time when I gather you;
    for I will make you renowned and praised
      among all the peoples of the earth,
    when I restore your fortunes
      before your eyes, says the LORD.

I started my exegetical process by exploring the text and noting observations, questions, or curiosities that came to mind. I noted such things as the following:

> This is the closing oracle of the book of Zephaniah. How does that
> position shape its use by the writer and its interpretation by the
> reader? I know little of either the prophet or the book of Zephaniah.
> I need to read to determine when this oracle was proclaimed/

written and if it fits (i.e., draws to a close) all of the material that precedes it. This is a short book, so it should be easy to answer these questions. (I realize part of my lack of familiarity with Zephaniah is that is it so poorly utilized by the RCL: 1:7,12–18 for Proper 28 Year A and 3:14–20 for Advent 3 Year C and all three years for the Easter Vigil.)

There are a number of places in the passage where the footnotes in the NRSV make it clear that there are serious textual and translation problems.

The language of restoration in this text reminds me of the language of Jeremiah 33.

This text is for the Third Sunday of Advent, traditionally Gaudete Sunday. So the RCL chose this text, at least in part, because of the call to rejoice.

There are a number of repetitions or parallels in the oracle:

Invitation to sing in v. 14 and God's singing in v. 17 (my mind goes to the special emphasis placed on music in Advent and Christmas);

Getting rid of the threat/results of disaster (vv. 15, 18);

God in our midst (vv. 15, 17) (my mind goes to the title Emmanuel assigned to Jesus in Matthew's infancy narrative).

The social justice language of reversal near the end of the passage is similar to what we will be hearing from Luke as we preach through it during Year C of the RCL.

I like the image of God bringing home in v. 20. Could this gathering image serve as a primary metaphor for the sermon? Does it imply that the oracle is postexilic? Does the "you" whom God will bring home refer to the oppressed in v. 19 or all of Israel/Jerusalem, whom the oracle addresses in the opening?

After this initial brainstorming, I turned to orient myself to Zephaniah more broadly. I glanced at a few commentaries' introductions to the book and then quickly skimmed through the three chapters that comprise the whole of Zephaniah (a task I could not have performed so easily if I were preaching on one of the longer prophetic books). The book opens by dating Zephaniah as prophesying during the reign of Josiah (640–609 BCE). While scholars have debated this dating, the final form of the book at least presents Zephaniah as offering his prophecies before or during Josiah's religious reform, since one of the things Zephaniah critiques is syncretism in Judah's religious practice. Indeed, the majority of the oracles of the book have a harsh tone of retribution. The day of the Lord will be a day of judgment on Judah/Jerusalem, on the nations, and indeed on the whole world. However, the end of the book turns more hopeful. In 3:8–13 the prophet proclaims that a faithful remnant will grow until all the peoples call on the name of the Lord. The book ends with an oracle that calls for rejoicing about this eschatological restoration (3:4–20).

The language in the last two oracles shifts from the earlier oracles' focus on the day of the Lord as judgment to a time of redemption:

> *the day* when I [God] arise as a witness (v. 8)
> *at that time* I will change the speech of the peoples to a pure speech (v. 9)
> *on that day* you shall not be put to shame (v. 11)
> *on that day* it shall be said to Jerusalem, "Do not fear," (v. 16)
> I will deal with all your oppressors *at that time* (v. 19)
> *at that time* I will bring you home (v. 20).

Some scholars argue that the radical change in tone from punishment in 1:2–3:7 to hope in 3:8–20 (and especially the tone of joy in vv. 14–20) indicates that these closing oracles have a different origin from the earlier ones. The language of gathering a remnant would suggest a postexilic context. But in its final form, the ending seems to present Zephaniah as prophesying about a future beyond the day of the Lord's wrath, that is, the even-more eschatological day of the Lord's redemption. This shift reminded me of Jeremiah's shift in tone that I struggled with in the sermon on 33:1–16.

I spent some time trying to get a sense of the structure and flow of the passage. Where is the emphasis or climax? Does any of the repetition of imagery signal movements? At first the passage didn't seem to exhibit much structure beyond beginning with an imperative—"Sing! Rejoice!" (v. 14)—which is followed by an offering of images of future salvation that justifies such exultation. But then I noticed that while there may not be an immediately obvious rhetorical structure, there is a temporal logic to the call to rejoice that is indicated by verb tense. The rationale for rejoicing begins in the past: "The LORD *has taken away* the judgments against you, he *has turned* away your enemies" (v. 15). It moves into the present: "The king of Israel, the LORD, *is* in your midst. . . ." (v. 15) and "The LORD, your God, *is* in your midst" (v. 17). Finally, the oracle ends in the eschatological future with the rest of the passage being filled out with verbs in the future tense: "will remove disaster" (v. 18), "will deal with oppressors . . .

will save the lame . . . will gather the outcast . . . will change shame into praise" (v. 19), "will bring you home . . . will make you renowned . . . will restore your fortunes" (v. 20).

In sum, then, Zephaniah's vision of God's future redemption is rooted in an experience of God as present in the present, which confirms that God has acted on our behalf in the past. I was struck by the idea that the claim that God is in our midst (indeed, in our troubled midst) implies hope for the future, even if there are signs of judgment all around. And this future hope demands rejoicing in the present.

Thursday, November 27
Review for Advent 1

Develop Focus & Imagery for Advent 2
I began the morning by returning to my sermon draft on Jer. 33:1–16 for the coming First Sunday of Advent. I read through it aloud, making a few editorial changes here and there, and I prepared the manuscript for the pulpit. This process helped me become familiar enough with the content of the sermon and its layout on paper so that when I step into the pulpit, the manuscript is a tool and not an anchor.

This took about 45 minutes, and then I was ready to return to my work on Mal. 2:17–3:5. With both the sermon on Jer. 33:1–16 and the exegetical work on Zeph. 3:14–20 on my mind, I was ready to determine a focus for the sermon for the Second Sunday of Advent. Advent 2 that year fell on the first Sunday of December, which, at Second Church, is the day we celebrate Holy Communion, and the liturgical movement from the sermon to the table usually shapes the imagery I use in the sermon on the first Sunday of the month. I began by reviewing my exegetical notes on the oracle and remembering that what grabbed me was the eschatological claim that the reformation of temple piety would precede social reform. Remembering what the text says paves the way for me to decide what I would say in my sermon.

Second Church is a community eager to both judge and influence society according to prophetic standards of justice. It is truly a community dedicated to addressing issues of peace and justice, but I wondered if the time had not come for us to reexamine our own practices to see if they were in accord with the very standards we held dear. Of course, this would be a natural part of the community's ongoing conversation about our future mission. But I thought it was important to name this aspect of our conversation in the pulpit and to name in worship the frustration of many that our invitations to those we serve to join us in community had rarely met a positive response.

So I took a stab at a sermonic focus: *Before the church can judge and transform the world, it must judge and transform itself.* As I reflected on this draft of a focus for my sermon, I felt uncomfortable because I did not want the focus to make us feel more frustrated or, worse, guilty about our failure. Rather, I wanted to move the congregation in a positive direction and shape a vision of hope like that with which this oracle ends. I tried to express myself in a more positive fashion: *When the church learns how to deal with the problems of the world that come inside from the outside, then what is going on inside our church will be a transforming model for what can happen out in the world.*

Still too negative. Once again: *As the church discovers more ways to embrace standards of peace and justice within its walls, it will be empowered to affect the world more significantly in terms of those standards.* This was better but still very broad. Although Malachi was not discussing issues of hospitality and acceptance of the other specifically, these had been recurring themes in Second Church's early discussion about its future direction. I needed to focus my scriptural lens better on this issue: *As the church discovers more ways to be inclusive in defining the boundaries of its community, it will be better empowered to address the marginalization of many that occurs in our society.* By using the words "more" and "better," this focus statement acknowledged both that the church was already working at being inclusive and addressing marginalization but that there was still work to be done. I was pleased that it moved from the broad structure of thought underlying the text from Malachi (i.e., temple reformation leads to societal reformation) to offering insight about a specific issue facing my congregation.

I rewrote this focus on the top of a new page in my notepad and began brainstorming for images, metaphors, and stories that related to this focus. I jotted down all kinds of things:

> At Second Church we take communion to those waiting in line outside for the soup kitchen to open after worship.
>
> Why does the church often seem to lag behind society in terms of social reform instead of leading the way?
>
> Fred Craddock tells a story of church that didn't open its doors to diversity and the building ended up being a restaurant where everyone was welcome.
>
> I will need to introduce Malachi to the congregation in the same way I sought an introduction.

If "Malachi" means "my messenger," is there a way Second Church should/could claim this as our name?

People can easily bring to mind images of exclusion. Can I provide strong, concrete images of inclusion?

A childhood experience at summer camp where an African American girl (she was one of only two African American children at the camp) pushed me to see her as a person instead of seeing her as a *black* person.

Recently at a restaurant I saw an elderly African American woman and an elderly Latino man sharing a meal: and we often characterize racism as a generational issue.

Deacon Burton's is a restaurant that everyone knows where poor and rich eat together at card tables. A friend likes to refer to the restaurant as the closest thing to the reign of God on earth.

A former white professor told of drinking water from a jug with African Americans for the first time at a civil rights gathering.

I need images where an example of inclusion transforms another situation:

Sesame Street models inclusion for children.

A man who was part of a church that struggled with the inclusion of homosexuals later established a policy extending health insurance benefits to domestic partners in his business.

A couple that had sent their children to private school to avoid racial problems in public schools later in life became advocates for methods of increasing diversity in schools when their son and his wife adopted a Vietnamese child.

Biblical images:

In Mark, Jesus curses the temple because it is not holding up to the standard of being a house of prayer for all nations.

Paul's use of the baptismal claim that there is neither Greek nor Jew. . . .

Conversion of the household of Cornelius in Acts

At the men's group, one white man shared his experience of growing up in the segregated south and then talked about how as an adult he struggled against his own prejudice but it seemed to pop up in his head against his will.

After writing down as many questions, ideas, stories, images, and metaphors as possible in the time I had set aside after reviewing this Sunday's sermon, I laid aside the focus and brainstorming notes to germinate until the beginning of the coming work week.

FRIDAY–SATURDAY, NOVEMBER 28–29
Days Off

SUNDAY, NOVEMBER 30
Preach on Advent 1
I preach the following sermon on Jer. 33:1–16:

No golden ball has dropped in Times Square. There was no *Dick Clark* special on television last night. We didn't toast one another with champagne or sing "Auld Lang Syne." There are no college football bowl games today. No ham and black-eyed peas to eat for good luck. But, nevertheless, for the church, today is New Year's Day.

We Christians are an odd lot. We mark time in a strange way. We don't set our spiritual clocks in accordance with the rotation of the earth on its axis or base our church calendar on the phases of the moon or determine our liturgical seasons in relation to the position of the earth in its rotation around the sun. Instead, we structure our worship time in accordance with ancient times. Our time is determined by Christ's time. We move from expectation to birth to revelation to baptism to transfiguration to ashes to temptation to crucifixion to resurrection to ascension until we receive the Spirit and celebrate the "ordinary" time of the church. And then we do it all over again: Advent to Christmas to Epiphany to Lent to Easter to Pentecost to Ordinary Time and back to Advent again.

We Christians mark time in a strange way. We use this cyclical practice of time to interpret the linear span of time in its entirety, from its beginning when the Spirit swept over the face of the formless void to its End (with a capital E) when the reign of God will be established as world without end. We use this cyclical practice of time to interpret *our* time as *God's* time, stretching from Alpha to us to Omega.

And what's even stranger is that each year we mark our beginning by looking ahead to the End (you know, that End with a capital E). God's End. The day of the Lord. For all the signs out there right now—sales in the department stores, decorations hanging from the lampposts, carols being played on the radio, and Santa sitting at his post at the mall—for all the signs of Christmas out there, we Christians say, "One thing at a time. Christmas will come soon enough. But right now is the beginning, which means it is time to think about the End." God's End. The day of Lord. The day God will come to us in a new way. That's what the word "advent" means—to come. We begin our year waiting, expecting, lifting up a vision of God coming to us in a manner that will be so new that time will never be the same again. So new that we can only talk about it as the End of what we know and experience now. As new as a babe born in Bethlehem was before we overexposed it.

That's where we begin the new year that the purple and the four-candled wreath signify—looking for God's new coming. But will we know it when we see it? I mean, what will it look like? Where do we find a vision of the End that is worthy of shaping the way we act and live in the world today? Where do we turn to find a vision of salvation that is worthy of describing it as God's advent?

How about the *Left Behind* series? It's pretty popular right now, wouldn't you say? This is a view of the End that has caught a great deal of attention. I must be honest, though; it hasn't caught mine. I haven't read a one of them. But I basically know the premillennial, dispensationalist view of the End that they contain, because when I was a teenager I remember attending a youth rally where they showed a film about the rapture. Some teenager was running through her house. The television that her father had been watching was still on. The blender was still running in the kitchen. But she was all alone. A narrator with a booming voice says, "If Frances had only given her life to Jesus, she would not have to face what was to come." And the film shifts to images of Frances with 666 on her forehead walking through what looked like what was left over after a nuclear bomb hit a sadomasochistic leper colony. This view of God's salvation that is yet to come is meant to, literally, scare the hell out of you. It is a literalist misunderstanding of the book of Revelation that strips that book of its evocative beauty and theological power.

So where do we turn to find a vision of salvation that is worthy of describing it as God's advent? Maybe we could turn to Jeremiah. Jeremiah offers a vision of God's coming that avoids the extreme of inciting fear. His vision is not a literal prediction of the End of the world, nor merely a description of the end of an individual life. It's a vision of the End (with a capital E)—the End of the status quo.

Jeremiah was an odd sort. He had been warning Judah that it was headed toward doom. Warning that Babylon was to conquer them as a sign of God's judgment. And then it happened. Just as he said. In 587

BCE, Babylon came and laid siege to Jerusalem. And in the narrative world of the book of Jeremiah, one of the king's first acts in response to the attack was to lock Jeremiah in prison.

But there, locked up in jail by his own king, with a foreign king's army beating down the city walls, days away from tearing down the temple and taking God's chosen people into exile, Jeremiah's tone changed. Instead of prophetically claiming, "Thus saith the LORD, 'I told you so,'" Jeremiah began speaking of God's salvation that would come. Now, mind you, he didn't have grand visions of Judah defeating Babylon. He didn't have some view of God swooping down out of the clouds to rescue the people at the last moment. His vision of God's coming, of God's salvation, was recovery after destruction hit. Salvation for Jeremiah was simply . . . *a return to normalcy.* Where there is desolation and despair, there will someday again be the normal activities of life. In place of piles of burnt rubble will be homes and farms. In the place of weeping will be people laughing on their way to a wedding or singing on their way to worship. In the place of a bottomed-out, stripped-out economy will be replenished flocks and herds. And in the place of inept, corrupt, oppressive rulers, God will cause a righteous Branch to spring up for David, who will act in ways that are just and right. There's no grand vision of a heaven on earth in this prophecy. No dirt roads becoming golden streets. No cities protected by pearly gates. There is the simple recognition that when life becomes a living hell, everyday normal activities can represent an experience of profound, divine grace.

If you're not sure you would count normalcy as salvation, ask anyone who has entered into remission after battling with cancer. Ask any woman who has gotten out of an abusive relationship. Or someone who has gotten a job after a time of being laid-off for six months. Or an alcoholic who is in recovery. Or someone who starts dating again after the dust of a bad marriage and a worse divorce has settled. Or a neighborhood that rebuilds after a tornado has torn it down. Or ask New York City if normal activities don't feel like saving grace in the aftermath of 9/11. As much as "reality" shows make it look like we long for thrills, romance, adventure, treasures, and so on and so forth, I think in a world where there is so much pain and turmoil and violence and poverty what we long for most deeply is for our reality to be normal. Jeremiah's is a great view of salvation: when God comes there will be an End (with a capital E) to hatred, oppression, sexism, ethnic cleansing, homelessness, war, and so on and so forth, and everything will just be normal.

But, come on—let's be honest. Aren't all those social evils I've listed (and the hundreds and thousands of others you could add to my lists)—aren't they all normal? Wasn't it Jesus who said, "You will always have the poor"? And isn't the whole reason we read Jeremiah as Scripture is that he was addressing a social reality that looks a lot like ours? Sure, the names in the newspaper articles are different, but twenty-six hundred years later the headlines are the same: somebody has stolen from someone else; someone has been found dead; some country invaded some smaller country; a bunch of people are out of work; and so on and so forth. The more things change, the more they stay the same. Isn't all the bad stuff in the world normal?

Well, we should be careful not to equate routine or habit with normalcy . . . especially with what is normal to God. Just because we get *used* to something, doesn't mean we should consider it normal. People may adapt to living without having enough food or adequate clothes or a decent home, but that way of life is *not* normal. We may be numb to the fact that to stretch our pennies we buy clothes made in sweat shops in Bangladesh and sold in discount stores by saleswomen who are not allowed to work full time so the stores can keep costs down and profits up by not paying health or retirement benefits, but that doesn't make it normal to use people that way. A community may get used to the idea that their water supply is filled with chemicals dumped into the river by a factory upstream, but that doesn't make the water normal. We may live in a society where thin and young are important values, but there is nothing normal about liposuction, Botox injections, breast implants, or face-lifts. We have gotten used to the idea that all politicians are corrupt, but that doesn't mean that we should hold political corruption as the norm. As residents in the United States we may be comfortable with the fact that we own 72 percent of the world's automobiles, 61 percent of the world's telephones, and 92 percent of the world's bathtubs while we only have 6 percent of the world's population, but that doesn't mean that that level of global inequity is normal. A child who has been burned with cigarettes regularly since she was an infant and grows up to marry a man who regularly gives her black eyes may think that that way of life is normal because she has never known anything different, but she would be wrong. Just because we have never known life without all of the awful injuries humanity inflicts on itself does not mean the way the world is is normal. At least not in God's eyes. Nor should it be considered normal by those who look for God in the world.

It's the First Sunday of Advent, New Year's Day for those of us who call ourselves Christian. So maybe we need to make some New Year's resolutions. We have begun at the End (with a capital E). We have begun with a vision of salvation, a vision of God coming to bring an End to all that is not normal. And we begin with that idealistic vision of God's future so we know how to lean into that future here and now. So that we can figure out ways to foreshadow God's standards for a normal world in the ways we interact with the world as individual Christians and as a church as a whole. So that we can be resolved to be agents of God's normalcy in a world of brokenness and chaos. When life becomes a living hell, everyday normal activities can represent an experience of profound, divine grace.

Do you remember a couple of years ago when Christmas fell on a Sunday? We struggled with what to do about our normal Sunday evening activities. It didn't feel right to cancel youth group, and youth choir rehearsal, and evening worship since it was one of the most holy days of the year. But after Christmas Eve and Christmas morning services, we knew attendance would be low. So somebody suggested that we have sort of a church family gathering and invite families from the nearby shelter for women and children to join us. We could have a simple meal and provide some presents for children and their mothers. It was a very special occasion, with children running all over the fellowship hall while adults sat around the table chatting about better days gone by and better days to come.

I remember especially, just before our guests got back on the vans to return to the shelter, one woman who came up to several of us. She was obviously about to thank us, but one of our members spoke up first: "Thank you for coming," he said. "You have a beautiful daughter, and your visit meant so much to us." The woman said, "Thank you for that. Oh, I appreciate the handbag for me and the toys for my girl. And the meal was delicious. But thank you mostly for helping the two of us feel normal again. It really does seem that Jesus has been born, doesn't it? Thank God for that."

When life becomes a living hell, everyday normal activities can represent an experience of profound, divine grace. Now that's a vision of salvation that is worthy of describing as God's advent.

MONDAY–TUESDAY, DECEMBER 1–2
Finish Developing Sermon for Advent 2
I returned now to my work on the sermon for the upcoming Second Sunday of Advent. The response I received to yesterday's sermon included

bland, "Nice sermon, Pastor" comments as people left the sanctuary, but a few engaged me in more significant conversation. More importantly, in a gathering Sunday evening that was a part of the ongoing conversation about the future of Second Church, two people referred to the sermon.

With these responses on my mind, I began this next task by reading aloud Mal. 2:17–3:5 and the focus statement. Then I skimmed my exegetical and brainstorming notes. Having reviewed text, interpretation, and possible imagery, I returned to consider whether my sermonic focus needed any further development. What I ended with on Thursday was, *As the church discovers more ways to be inclusive in defining the boundaries of its community, it will be better empowered to address the marginalization of many that occurs in our society.* Part of the previous evening's conversation had centered on the desire to bridge the gap between the soup kitchen and other outreach ministries, on the one hand, and the rest of what goes on in the church, on the other. Someone had mentioned that he really appreciated our taking communion outside to the people standing in line for the soup kitchen and what a powerful experience it was for him to be a chalice bearer for those outside. I was reminded that I had thought of this as a positive image while brainstorming on Thursday, but another woman responded that, while she too appreciated that this was our practice having had the opportunity to serve outside has made her feel uncomfortable (even guilty) receiving communion inside. She asked, "Is some being served outside while others eat inside really communion?" The longer the conversation went on, the more it confirmed for me what we all already knew: Second Church is a white, middle-class church. And although we have made many invitations, we have only been minimally successful at welcoming African Americans and persons of lower economic status who live near the church into our faith community.

I decided to struggle with this specific issue in my sermon, and I changed my focus to be slightly more explicit: *As Second Church discovers more ways to be inclusive of persons with less means and of African Americans, it will be better empowered to address the marginalization of many that occurs in our society.* In my earlier brainstorming, I had been thinking of "the church" in more general terms and had thought that by addressing the general issue of extending church boundaries, Second Church members could plug in our own situation as they listened. The rising level of anxiety I had heard at Sunday evening's gathering, however, led me now to address more narrowly this congregation's issues. I needed to be careful that while I called us to look for new ways to be more inclusive, I did not simply raise the anxiety level another notch. I wanted to be pastoral—celebrating the many ways we have tried (sometimes succeeding) to be more inclusive, claiming as my own the congregation's frustration over failures, and providing some sort of (eschatological) vision of moving beyond our current situation.

After fine-tuning the focus, I spent more time brainstorming. This time I tried to think about and remember ways in which Second Church had been or failed to be inclusive and how it might be more inclusive. I came up with the following:

> Our music reflects the heritage of classical, European "sacred" music, and the liturgy and my preaching reflect the style of white, middle-class mainline Protestantism. We have invited others to join us, but how must we change for them to be truly welcomed in worship (and other areas of the church)? How much are we willing to change?
>
> Could I create an image where those on the soup line are serving us food and nurturing us? Would this lead to a vision of us sharing a meal in the world instead of us providing a meal for them in the soup kitchen. (Play with this image more later: it might work as a good conclusion, since we are celebrating the Eucharist on Sunday and will be taking it out to the line.)
>
> Much of the neighborhood around the church is subsidized housing and is populated with African Americans who live near and below the poverty line. Most of our congregation drives past this neighborhood from the suburbs as they come to this downtown church.
>
> We have allowed various cultural and political events to take place in our sanctuary that have brought a wide range of people into our building.
>
> Soup kitchen volunteers always sit and eat *with* our guests once the rush is over.
>
> A number of our regular soup kitchen volunteers know a number of our regular homeless guests by name. And some members mention seeing guests during the week and speaking with them on the street.
>
> People come inside from the soup line during worship time if the weather is inclement.

I also spent some of this brainstorming time thinking about the form this sermon should take. Instead of providing vocabulary to resource the broad conversations going on at Second Church, I had chosen to address a very particular element of the current conversation. And since I was going to address it directly, I needed to use a sermonic flow that would allow me to present my focus clearly and to explore its implications. But I also needed to take into consideration that the congregation probably had little knowledge of Malachi. So I decided that the classic and straightforward form of exegesis/interpretation/application would serve well if adapted a little:

> *Introduction*: I would begin with some comments commending the congregation for how the conversation about the church's future was going and describe some of its impact on me, including the way I listened to the Bible as I prepare for preaching.
>
> *Exegesis*: Then I would introduce Malachi and walk through 2:17–3:5, showing how language of temple reform and social reform are related.
>
> *Interpretation*: This view of the passage would lead to a theological statement similar to my broader focus statement, i.e., that as the modern church opens itself to reform, it will be better able to transform society.
>
> *Application*: At this point I would narrow our focus to Second Church's struggle to be inclusive in its community and to bring those who are marginalized toward the center of society. This last section should not result in a list of "oughts" but in an honest appraisal of the church's struggle (failures and successes) and a vision of hope for the future.

Once a sermon draft is fully written, I lay it aside until Thursday.

WEDNESDAY, DECEMBER 3
Exegesis for Advent 4

With the sermon on Malachi written and fresh in my mind, I turn to exegesis of the text for the final Sunday in Advent. A little farther back, but not too distant in my mind, was the sermon I preached three days earlier on Jeremiah. Beginning to work on the sermon for the Fourth Sunday of Advent so soon after preaching on the First Sunday and writing the sermon for the Second Sunday, helped me think about the season's continuity from beginning to end. Yet I was also aware that this last Advent service, more than the others, bridges the gap between expectation and fulfillment, between eschatology and incarnation, between Advent and

Christmas. And thus I was glad that the church staff chose to shift from the Old Testament Prophets to the prophetic utterance of Mary in Luke 1:39–56. This choice would prepare the congregation to hear Luke 2:1–20 read on Christmas Eve.

I was also aware that 1) this was the first time I would be preaching on Luke in the new lectionary cycle and 2) this sermon should connect with the adult Sunday school class in which I introduced Luke, for they will continue to discuss the Gospel in detail. Having just led discussions of the Gospel as a whole and being generally more familiar with Luke–Acts than with the prophetic texts I was preaching on during the rest of Advent, I did not expect exegesis to be as difficult as it had been for the other three sermons. So I began, first reading through the text and then jotting down initial impressions:

1:39 In those days Mary set out and went with haste to a Judean town in the hill country, 40 where she entered the house of Zechariah and greeted Elizabeth. 41 When Elizabeth heard Mary's greeting, the child leaped in her womb. And Elizabeth was filled with the Holy Spirit 42 and exclaimed with a loud cry, "Blessed are you among women, and blessed is the fruit of your womb. 43 And why has this happened to me, that the mother of my Lord comes to me? 44 For as soon as I heard the sound of your greeting, the child in my womb leaped for joy. 45 And blessed is she who believed that there would be a fulfillment of what was spoken to her by the Lord." 46 And Mary said,

"My soul magnifies the Lord,
47   and my spirit rejoices in God my Savior,
48   for he has looked with favor on the lowliness of his servant.
         Surely, from now on all generations will call me blessed;
49   for the Mighty One has done great things for me,
         and holy is his name.
50   His mercy is for those who fear him
         from generation to generation.
51   He has shown strength with his arm;
         he has scattered the proud in the thoughts of their hearts.
52   He has brought down the powerful from their thrones,
         and lifted up the lowly;
53   he has filled the hungry with good things,
         and sent the rich away empty.
54   He has helped his servant Israel,
         in remembrance of his mercy,

> [55] according to the promise he made to our ancestors,
>   to Abraham and to his descendants forever."
> [56] And Mary remained with her about three months and then
>   returned to her home.

Immediately I recognized some of the broad Lukan themes we had been discussing in Sunday school:

> The subordination of John to Jesus throughout the infancy narrative.
> The lifting up of women more than in the other Gospels.
> Prophetic characterization related to ecstatic utterance and being filled with the Spirit.
> Salvation as the reversal of status quo, especially in terms of economic status and power.
> The emphasis on God's fulfilling promises made to Israel in the Christ Event and the beginnings of the Church.

I called to mind some of Luke's differences with the other Synoptic Gospels. While Mark does begin with John as a precursor to Jesus, the earliest Gospel has no infancy narrative at all. Matthew, on the other hand, includes an infancy narrative, but John the Baptist is not part of it. Moreover, in Matthew's infancy narrative, Joseph is the key parent instead of Mary. Mary never speaks in Matthew, and yet here in Luke she offers the opening prophetic speech that sets the tone for the whole Gospel, indeed in some sense the tone for all of Luke–Acts.

As I dug into exegesis with the other Advent sermons on my mind, I decided that I wanted this sermon to focus primarily on the Magnificat instead of the narrative of Mary and Elizabeth's visit. In the sermon, I would want to refer to the narrative setting and indeed the broader narrative context of the infancy narrative to help establish a connection between the Fourth Sunday of Advent and Christmastide, but having dealt with prophetic oracles for the first three weeks of Advent, I decided to focus on Mary's prophetic utterance as well (in line with the original reason we chose this text).

The Magnificat speaks of what God *has done*. But the past tense is in reality a prophetic idiom that expresses a view of the future, that is, an eschatological vision. This text, therefore, speaks about what God *is going to do* through the one soon to be born. And, although it is usually ignored amid the sentimentalizing of Christmas, the incarnation has radical political and economic implications. And this would be the focus of my sermon.

THURSDAY, DECEMBER 4
Review for Advent 2

Develop Focus & Imagery for Advent 3

I began my morning by reviewing and rehearsing my sermon on Mal. 2:17–3:5 for the Second Sunday of Advent. I found a number of places where the wording was awkward and might not convey what I intended, but overall the sermon "felt" good to me. I corrected the minor problems, got the manuscript into a format ready for the pulpit, and printed it out for Sunday.

Then I picked up my exegetical notes on Zeph. 3:14–20 for the Third Sunday of Advent to remind myself what I had heard in the text and to choose the focus of what aspect of God's hide-and-seek presence I would give witness to in this sermon. After a series of judgment oracles, the book of Zephaniah ends with a call to rejoicing. The people are to rejoice because just as God has been with them in the past and is present now even in the midst of distress, God will be with them in the future and bring salvation.

I wanted to create a sermon that had this same basic focus and led the people to a sense of celebration and hope: *The experiences of God's presence in our past and present offer a vision of God's future redemption.* To pull this sermon off, I would need to gather images of individual's and community's past and present experiences of God and find a way to say, "How much more there is to come!" But I wanted to do this without denying experiences of God's judgment and of God as distant or absent. So I brainstormed and came up with a list of ideas:

> The difference between the way I felt God's presence as an adolescent (conversing with God and telling God jokes at bedtime) to now when God seems awfully silent at times.
>
> Special worship services at Second Church (especially Christmas services): It would be good to celebrate worship at Second Church in this Advent 3 sermon, since in the Advent 2 sermon I will be challenging us think about the way worship excludes some from experiencing God's presence.
>
> Prayer concerns in worship: how people lift up incidents of suffering in the world due to violence, prejudice, illness, hatred, loneliness, etc. This holds in tension God's silence (seen in the problems mentioned in prayer) and God's presence (seen in the people's concern for one another and in expectation of God's healing).
>
> Altar-call experiences that for many people become paradigmatic. On the other hand, Langston Hughes has a short story about

an altar call at which he waited for Jesus to come but Jesus didn't.

Church near the interstate in Atlanta that has ugly neon sign on steeple that says JESUS SAVES. Sign may be ugly, but no one would notice the church if it weren't for that sign. And now as people head here, there, or nowhere, they can't help but catch a glimpse of this neon witness of God's presence.

I remembered that I am drawn to the imagery of ingathering at the end of the passage and searched for imagery of God's presence related to this:

Each year Second Church has a homecoming where former pastors and members are invited back to celebrate the history of the church and what it has meant in the lives of so many people who worshiped here and the ministry it has had in this city. This image celebrates God's presence in our past, and since the service is a high moment of each year, it also celebrates God's presence in the present. A description of these services could be shaped in a way to point to the future. What would a story-sermon about an Advent homecoming service based on this text sound like?

The beginning of the order of worship in our bulletin each week has the heading "Gathering," which is followed by Proclamation, Response, and Sending Forth. Gathering to worship in the midst of all of the ills of today's world is a powerful witness to God's presence in the midst of brokenness.

As my designated sermon preparation time drew to a close, I read back over my brainstorming and realized three things about the directions my thoughts had gone: 1) there were no images that build well on the social justice themes of the previous two Sundays in Advent; 2) I was especially attracted to the story by Langston Hughes; and 3) I also liked the possibility of developing a story-sermon related to an Advent Homecoming. I laid aside my notes to give them a chance to settle over the weekend and would see what I was thinking and feeling on Monday.

FRIDAY–SATURDAY, DECEMBER 5–6
Days Off

SUNDAY, DECEMBER 7
Preach on Advent 2
I preach the following sermon on Mal. 2:17–3:5:

I probably don't say enough how privileged I feel to serve as your pastor and how proud I am of the ministry of this church. When white flight brought about the death of so many downtown churches here, Second Church retooled and found an important voice to address urban social issues. And now, even though we are not facing that kind of crisis, you have nevertheless taken it upon yourself to retool again so that you find more ways to be in relevant ministry in the name of Jesus Christ.

I am so excited and inspired by the conversations we have been having about the future of this congregation. I'll admit that even though we are still near the beginning, they are at moments quite painful. And I assume as we get deeper and deeper in the conversation and move to the point of making some decisions, we'll have some significant disagreements. But to be a part of a community that is willing to face such struggles openly, honestly, and prayerfully fills me with great hope.

It's hard to express just how much of an impact this process is having on me as your pastor. Every task I do in the church right now is shaped by our conversations. Especially preaching. Every time I turn to a new biblical passage for a new Sunday, I ask myself, How does this relate to what we are discussing, to who we have been and who we want to become?

Take this week's Scripture lesson, for instance. The Second Sunday of Advent usually focuses on John the Baptist as the one who prepares the way for Jesus' coming, for the advent of Jesus' ministry. And, indeed, the passage we read from Malachi was interpreted by the ancient church as a prediction of John the Baptist: "I am preparing my messenger to prepare the way before me. . . ." Now, modern interpreters have long since abandoned reading the Old Testament Prophets as if they were fortunetellers predicting the future. They understand them to have been sociotheological analysts who commented on and suggested courses of action for the political, social, and religious institutions of the day in the name of Yahweh, the God of Israel and Judah. But in the context of Advent the church still often uses the passage to help them understand the early church's understanding of Jesus' precursor. For me, though, it was less the story of John the Baptist that defined the way I listened to this passage and more our conversation about the future of Second Church.

Outside of the book of Malachi, we know nothing of an ancient prophet named Malachi. Because the oracles of this short book critique temple practice, most scholars assume that the prophecies come from a time after Jews had returned from the Babylonian exile and after the temple had been reconstructed. This would be about seventy years or so after the first temple had been destroyed and then rebuilt and about five hundred years before Christ was born. Just because temple worship had retooled itself after the exile doesn't mean it didn't need to be reformed and purified from time to time.

In our passage Malachi accuses the people of wearying God with questions about whether God favors those who are evil since evil people seem to prosper. "Where is the God of justice?" they ask. And Malachi provides God's answer, an Advent answer: "I am coming. And when I come I will purify the temple and then I will address social injustices." Now, Malachi is a pretty short book: a total of only six prophetic oracles. So why didn't he take more time and elaborate? Why didn't he preach one sermon about the temple and another about social ills? By bringing these two issues together, Malachi is trying to show that religious life and cultural life are inseparable. He is trying to say that social injustice results from religious impiety. Or to put it positively, the prophet implies that religious reform will lead to social reform.

You know, denomination after denomination spends a great deal of energy worrying about decreasing membership, and preacher after preacher stands in the pulpit decrying the loss of values in society and the terrible oppression that can be found everywhere. But how often do we hear the two concerns connected? How often do we hear the church asking, "What needs to change inside our walls before the world can change out there?" If the church wants to have a prophetic voice that can help reform the world, then we need to open ourselves to reform first. We need to get the log out of our eye before we try to get the speck out of the world's.

Now, surely when we talk about the need for the church to reform so that social problems can be addressed, we're not talking about Second Church. We're talking about our denomination that has become an institution, which is an end unto itself. Or we're talking about churches in the suburbs that have become like country clubs with chaplains. But not us. We talk about the poor and the oppressed and the marginalized constantly. We support a variety of community ministries, including a soup kitchen, counseling services for victims of drug addiction, shoes for the homeless, and family gatherings for those living in shelters during the holidays. We have conversations about government decisions that we want to support and decisions that we think are unjust. We have let needed repairs on our building go undone so that we might use our resources to better care for those in need. And every first Sunday of the month, like today, we take communion out to the people in line for Sunday dinner so that we can offer them the hospitality of Christ. A friend of mine likes to kid me and call our church "The Church of the Liberal Bleeding Heart Jesus." What about us could need reforming?

And yet, that is the question at the root of our conversations right now. That's why I am so excited and inspired by the conversations we have been having about the future of this congregation. We're not just talking about how to get more people in the pews, how to increase the bottom line of our budget, or how to build a new family life center. We are a congregation that is attempting to be a Malachi unto itself and to ask seriously and honestly, What about us needs reforming so that we can better transform the world?

One of the partial answers to that question keeps coming up as a theme in our conversations. We have especially focused on it this last week, although it's something we have talked about long before these formal conversations began. It is our frustration with ministering *to* those who live around the church but not finding ways to be in ministry *with* them. It's the desire to do a better job of connecting our worshiping community and the communities we aid in our outreach ministries. We are a predominantly white, middle-class congregation set in the middle of an area that is predominantly populated by African Americans who are struggling economically. We have invited our neighbors in, but for some reason or another, in spite of our good intentions, we have been unsuccessful in making them feel at home. I am convinced that as Second Church discovers more ways to be inclusive of our neighbors, we will be better empowered to address the marginalization of those neighbors by society.

Now, I wish I had a solution for how we do that, how we become more inclusive internally as well as in our outreach ministries. How our intent to be inclusive becomes actual inclusivity. But I don't. And maybe it's too early for that. Maybe it's too early in our conversations for us to begin proposing any specific solutions. After all, we are only in the stage of identifying our concerns and beginning to shape a broad vision of where we would like to be over against those concerns. And I think I can contribute to that level of conversation right now.

I feel like we have tried very hard to invite our neighbors to join in community with us. And I celebrate our attempts. But I wonder, from the perspective of our neighbors, do our invitations feel like an invitation from my wife's great-aunt, who would say how glad she was to have visitors only to constantly remind the children that they weren't allowed to touch anything in the house. I wonder if we have invited neighbors in but have unintentionally said to them, "You are welcome here as long as you don't touch anything important."

I mean, look at worship as an example. We have been very intentional about not making the sanctuary feel pristine in any way so that if any of our homeless neighbors wanted to come to worship just to be out of the cold, they would feel comfortable in the environment. But what will they hear and see in worship, if they do come to get warmed? They will hear hymns and anthems that we love, but which reflect the heritage of classical, European "sacred" music. They will read a liturgy that echoes the great Western traditions of formal, exalted worship language. And they will hear a sermon from me that will reflect a style that has shaped me, but is narrowly white, middle-class, mainline preaching. A question we have to ask as part of our forward-looking conversation is, How can we change worship so that the music and the prayers and the proclamation include our neighbors instead of requiring great adaptation on their part? How do we make significant changes to be more hospitable to newcomers of different ethnic and socioeconomic backgrounds than most of us without in turn making those of us who have been here a while not feel like strangers in a foreign land?

Well, as I said, I don't have a solution, and it's too early in our conversations to be proposing specific actions we should be taking. I do believe, however, that as we move toward such solutions together, this church will be better equipped to break down the barriers that marginalize our neighbors in society. And while I don't know how to make that happen just yet, I can imagine what it looks like. I'll bet it looks a little like this one restaurant in the deep South did one Friday night. This restaurant memorializes much of the racism that defined the South. The manager and the cashier are white, while those who wait tables, prepare the food, and clear tables are all African American. In fact, the waitresses all dress in Mammy outfits.

Well, this one Friday night, a Quaker youth choir on tour was eating there. And after their meal, these white, middle-class youth on vacation offered to sing a song for the restaurant. But in payment they required that someone sing a song for them in return. When an agreement was reached, the choir, all dressed in their uniforms—something like blue blazers, oxford shirts, and khaki slacks—organized themselves in lines and began singing "Amazing Grace." They sang in perfect four-part harmony with all voices exactly in tune, everyone keeping exactly the right tempo and rhythm. While they sang, customers put down their beer and pushed aside their fried chicken; and when the choir finished everyone in the restaurant exploded in applause.

Then it was the restaurant's turn to sing to the choir. An African American woman had come out from the kitchen. Her job was to make the drop biscuits that came with every meal that was served. So she was wearing a hairnet and an apron and was covered with flour. And she began to sing. She, too, sang "Amazing Grace." Only her voice was not classically trained. With the crisp notes of the youth choir still echoing in the rafters, she slid from one note to another, she changed tempo here and there, she slurred words together, and she altered her rhythm freely. To be the same song, it was amazingly different. And yet it was just as beautiful. It is rare to be able to hear a solo by Gabriel right after hearing an angel choir. The customers' food had grown cold by now, but no one cared. They clapped until their hands hurt, because they had been fed by two radically different renditions of the same hymn that merged into a single experience of beauty and of community. For just a moment the beer and biscuits was replaced with bread and wine. For just a moment, a bunch of strangers, black and white, became church.

"I am sending my messenger to prepare the way before me, and the Lord whom you seek will suddenly come . . . the Lord whom you seek will suddenly come . . . to his temple."

MONDAY–TUESDAY, DECEMBER 8–9
Finish Developing Sermon for Advent 3

Although I intentionally ended yesterday's sermon on Mal. 2:17–3:5 with an image that was meant to offer hope in the midst of the recognition that change is needed not only in our culture but in our congregation, the sermon felt "heavy" to me. No one took offense at the direction I was pushing the congregation in this contribution to our ongoing conversations. Indeed, one of the few African American members of the church shook my hand and thanked me for acknowledging her need to be included. But a few white members shared their recognition that if we moved the way I suggested, they would be less comfortable in worship with words such as "You hit the nail on the head; I'm just afraid it's my head," and "Well, I guess there's no turning back now."

This weight made me want to reclaim the call to rejoice as central to the Third Sunday of Advent even more than I did when I first began thinking about Zeph. 3:14–20, but I didn't want it to be joyfulness that denied the weightiness of the issues facing us. I wanted to remind this congregation that it had much to celebrate about the ways it had been a witness to God's real presence in the world, and, indeed, I wanted to begin foreshadowing the joy of Immanuel, God-with-us.

Even though I had taken Friday and Saturday off, I actually spent a fair amount of informal time over the weekend reflecting on the idea of a story-sermon about an Advent Homecoming service. In the process, I remembered that last Advent I had preached a story-sermon on the Magnificat, which was to be the text used in the Advent 4 service.

I began now to formalize some of the ideas that had been floating around in my head by writing them down and sifting through them:

> Why would a homecoming service be set during Advent instead of spring or fall? It could be a special anniversary celebrating the founding of the church.
>
> Exegesis helped me see a structure of past, present, and future in the text. The three perspectives should play a role in the narrative structure of my story-sermon. 1) Someone in the congregation should be the historian who recites God's presence with and through the church in the past. Perhaps an old man who was present at the founding. 2) Perhaps the goal of the homecoming service is to look back, but in reality the congregation begins to look forward (to God's coming presence). 3) Maybe the past, present, and future dimensions could be represented by three generations within a family; e.g., the old man, his son, and a granddaughter.
>
> For the story to work, a conflict of some sort is needed to which a resolution is provided. Perhaps the old man is to speak about the past of the church but dies just before the homecoming service. Problem: the conflict must not weigh down the story so much that it cannot be pulled back up to an invitation to rejoice. So after mourning the loss of the old man, the congregation must somehow be invited to identify with the granddaughter.

I played with these ideas on Monday, and by Tuesday I was ready to write. When I sat at the computer, a story flowed out that I felt grew out of my interpretation of the Zephaniah passage and pointed back to it, and which offered hope (in a narrative fashion) for the future of Second Church as it decided what to leave behind and what to carry forward.

Wednesday, December 10
Exegesis for Christmas 1

I turned now to the task of exegesis for the First Sunday after Christmas. Because Epiphany (January 6) fell early in the week, the staff had decided to celebrate Epiphany Sunday on January 4. In turn, we decided to use the Gospel lection (John 1:1–18) assigned for the Second Sunday after Christmas for the First Sunday after Christmas in order to continue to focus on the theme of incarnation from Christmas Eve. Thus I spent the morning exploring John's *logos* theology for describing the preexistence and coming of Christ.

Thursday, December 11
Review for Advent 3

Develop Focus & Imagery for Advent 4

I returned to my story-sermon manuscript for the coming Sunday (Third Sunday of Advent), made some minor changes in character description, sharpened the ending a little, and prepared my pulpit version.

This took less than a half hour, so I turned my attention to determining my focus for the Fourth Sunday of Advent fairly quickly. I reviewed my exegetical notes on Luke 1:39–56. Having just completed a sermon on a text from Zephaniah that dealt with past, present, and future perspectives, I was drawn back to the eschatological use of the past tense in the Magnificat: Luke presents Mary as speaking of what God *has done* in order to foreshadow/prophesy what God is *going to do* through the one to whom she is going to give birth. Indeed, I was reminded of one of the primary reasons this text was suggested by the music minister in the first place: by placing the Magnificat alongside readings from Jeremiah, Malachi, and Zephaniah, Mary is presented as a prophet. And what Mary, the prophet, claims (and thus what Luke, the author, claims) with such eschatological certainty that God is going to do through Christ is to show mercy to those who fear God and scatter the proud of heart; bring down the powerful from their thrones; and lift up the lowly, fill the hungry, and send the rich away empty.

I began to develop a sermonic focus that could bring the time dimension and the social understanding of salvation together. I went through several focus statements, struggling with wording that is precise and comfortable, and I came up with the following: *We retell the ancient story of Christ's coming into the world in order to envision a just future for the world.*

With a focus statement in hand, I moved to brainstorming for imagery and ideas that would help unpack my focus and help me decide where to go with it. I began by seeking analogies of looking back and looking forward:

> Do genealogists get a sense of who they are by looking back at their ancestors?
>
> Second Church's conversation strategy of older members sharing their memories before we turn to conversations about where we should be headed.
>
> The story-sermon on Zephaniah that begins in the past and moves into the future.
>
> Joke: "An economist is an expert who will know tomorrow why the things he predicted yesterday did not happen today."[3]
>
> Biblical models: 1) Recurring use of exodus motif to describe God's coming salvation. 2) Language in the Apocalypse that is taken from Daniel to help interpret the present church's view of the future. 3) Midrash.
>
> Those who do not learn from history are destined to repeat it.
>
> Dickens' *A Christmas Carol*—Ghosts of Christmas Past, Present, and Future.
>
> Going back and rereading an early section of a novel (e.g., a mystery) to catch foreshadowing you missed originally and help you figure out where the plot is going.

I also explored the reversal imagery, looking for modern parallels:

> Those listed as the richest in *Forbes* magazine will trade places with residents in the federal housing projects surrounding Second Church. Or those in the suburbs will trade places with those in the urban housing projects.
>
> Those who throw away food ("daily bread") that spoils in their fridge will be hungry and those who eat food thrown into dumpsters will be filled with Christmas feasts (messianic feasts).
>
> Those who hoard lots of money that says "In God we trust" will be scattered and those who pray that God help them make it from paycheck to paycheck will receive mercy.
>
> Those above the glass ceiling will be brought down and those below the poverty line will be lifted up.

Also, to try to get my creative juices flowing, I played with language for a sermon introduction that might raise the issue of the past tense at the same time that it presents Mary as a prophet:

Mary must have been absent the day they studied verb tense in grammar school. She has just come to visit her kinswoman Elizabeth. Elizabeth and John in Elizabeth's womb recognize and rejoice that Mary is pregnant with God's only begotten child. Mary joins in their rejoicing by uttering what is traditionally called the Magnificat—called this because she starts with the words "My soul *magnifies* the Lord." In this poetic speech she praises God for what God is going to do through the child she is carrying inside her. But this is where the problem arises. She is talking about what God is going to do, but she speaks in the past tense. Best I can figure out, either Mary just never studied verb tense . . . or she was a prophet.

Following in the line of prophets like Jeremiah, Malachi, and Zephaniah, Mary speaks with the confidence of one to whom God has revealed God's purposes. So confident that she speaks of what God is going to do through Jesus in language of God having already done it:

His mercy is for those who fear him
   from generation to generation.
He has shown strength with his arm;
   he has scattered the proud in the thoughts of their hearts.
He has brought down the powerful from their thrones,
   and lifted up the lowly;
he has filled the hungry with good things,
   and sent the rich away empty.

(Luke 1:50–53)

Looking over these lines, I realized that were I to use this kind of language for the sermon opening, I would have to decide how to transition to what would come next. The more I reflected on this, the less it felt like it would work. So I turned toward a more inductive design for the sermon:

Opening question: "How do we determine what the future should look like?"

Answer: Mary's prophecy points us to look at what God has done in the past.

Conclusion: Therefore, with the fourth candle of the wreath lit, we should look at what God did in Christ's coming into the world in order to envision a just future for the world.

As my morning study time drew to a close, I laid this work aside to return to it at the beginning of next week.

SUNDAY, DECEMBER 14
Preach on Advent 3
I preach the following story-sermon on Zeph. 3:14–20, entitled "Past, Present, and Future":

One of the best things about growing up in Tinyville, Mississippi, was Little Zeph. His full name was Zephaniah Lucretius Harper, III. The only reason I knew his full name was because of the universal law that mothers are required to use their children's full names when angry at them. If my mama was a little mad she would just use my first and last name, "Jackson Hillman, what am I going to do with you?" But if she was really mad she would throw in that middle name for emphasis: "Jackson Lewis Hillman, you'd better quit that or start running and never turn back."

My mama had plenty of good reason to yell at me, I guess, but I was an angel compared to Little Zeph. His mother was constantly yelling something like "Zephaniah Lucretius Harper, III, you better get right with God this instant or you are going to know what the judgment of God feels like up close and personal!" She yelled at him constantly because he was constantly doing something he shouldn't. This kid was always starting fights at school. He hid in the bushes and scared old women when they walked by. Heck, his favorite hobby was throwing rocks at kittens.

Little Zeph and I were good friends, and many were the times that I followed him a far piece down the road to hell. But I idolized him, because wherever I chickened out and refused to go any further, he was just getting started. What's not there for a nine-year-old boy to love and respect?!

I know we were nine because it was 1902, the year Resurrection Methodist Episcopal Church South was celebrating its seventy-fifth anniversary. It was a big deal in our little town. To celebrate, the church had planned a homecoming service, based on the scriptural theme "At that time I will bring you home, at the time when I gather you in; for I will make you renowned and praised among all the peoples of the earth." Members of the church who had moved away were invited back. Former pastors were returning to offer prayers for the congregation. And the other churches in town had agreed to join us for worship. Now, in Tinyville, Mississippi, around the turn of the century there were only three churches. There was the Methodist church, the Baptist church, and the black church. It was rare enough to have Methodists and Baptists worship together, but to have whites and blacks join together in praise and prayer and proclamation was equivalent to the End of time (with a capital E).

The homecoming service was to take place in December, because that's when the church got started. You see, a traveling Methodist evangelist had come through the area that December of 1827 and held a tent meeting. The handful of people who were living in the area at the time were moved by the services and decided to start a church. And the first act of the church was to baptize a young boy and bring him into the faith. That first boy to be baptized was now the only founding member of the church still alive for the seventy-fifth anniversary, and his name was Zephaniah Lucretius Harper (the First). So in 1902, there were three generations of Zephaniahs in Resurrection Church. To keep them straight, everybody called Zephaniah Sr., "Mr. Harper"; everybody called Jr., "Zephaniah"; and everybody called the Third, "Little Zeph."

The reason I knew how the church got started, of course, was that Mr. Harper was constantly telling Little Zeph and his friends about the history of the church. And he especially made us listen to his stories as the anniversary drew near, because the church had asked him to be the keynote speaker. Mr. Harper's sermon was going to celebrate the many ways God had been present with and through Resurrection Church throughout all its days.

He rehearsed on us boys. He told us about how Resurrection Church built the first church building in the area and later was the first church in rural Mississippi to have a stained-glass window installed in the sanctuary. He told about great-camp meetings where people were called to repentance and invited to give their lives to Christ. He told about ways the church had helped out poor dirt farmers on occasion when the harvest wasn't very good, about how it had supported women and children who had become widows and orphans due to the Civil War.

And whenever he mentioned the Civil War—and he always called it the "Civil War" even though there were plenty of people in Mississippi who either called it the War between the States or the War of Northern Aggression—he would say, "Well, you can't talk about the way God has been present with the church and the way God has been present through the church without confessing that there were times that the church was unfaithful, and God judged us for it." And then he would tell about the split in the Methodist Episcopal Church in the mid-1840s. And he would say, "People still like to claim that the split was about the authority of the bishop or the power of the General Conference, but it was really about one thing and one thing only: slavery. And we were on the wrong side of the argument. No church can be true to the life and death and resurrection of Jesus Christ and at the same time support one people owning and using another people." If he stopped there, you would be just as depressed as you could be. But he didn't. He would smile a little smile of hope and say, "Of course, the story don't end there. After the war was over, plenty of white folks was even worse to the Blacks than they were when they was slaves. But Resurrection Church felt bad about its complicity in the sin of slavery. Nothing could make up for the past, but the church did try and do some good. We raised the money to build the black church and to pay the black preacher until the church could get on its own feet. And we gave lots of support to Miss Janie, the white woman who turned her plantation house into an orphanage for black children who were left without parents or owners after the war."

Mr. Harper would go on and tell stories about special worship services, sponsoring of missionaries, some of the boys the church sent off into the ministry, and so on and so forth. And he would always end his storytelling session by saying something like, "We are a bunch of lousy sinners here at Resurrection Church. But isn't it something to be joyful about that God has taken away our judgment and even found ways to use us to begin turning the tables around!"

I tell you what, Mr. Harper was eighty-four years old, but he was as excited as a schoolboy about the homecoming service. But then again, so was his schoolboy grandson. Little Zeph had a plan. He felt like the anniversary service represented an opportunity unlike any other that had ever presented itself for him to display his talents. He asked me to help him, but I knew that if I messed around in church, especially at this service, my mama would do a lot more to me than just use my full name. But even though I wasn't going to help, I was in awe of his ambition and asked him what he was going to do. And he said, "Well, you know, as part of his sermon, Gramps is going to talk about judgment and all the way he always does. So I thought I would help him out with a miniature plague on Egypt. I've been going down to the marsh every chance I get to collect frogs. I've got almost a hundred. I haven't figured out just how yet, but right when Gramps gets to the part about judgment, I'm going to release those frogs into the sanctuary!"

I couldn't wait to see what would happen come Sunday. But I never got the chance. Unexpected to everyone, a few days before the homecoming service, Mr. Harper died. He just passed away as peaceful as could be in his sleep. We had the funeral on Saturday morning, but I didn't hear a word the preacher said. I guess nine-year-olds rarely listen to what preachers have to say, especially at funerals. But it wasn't just being nine that kept me from listening. It was the sight of Little Zeph. He sat on his mama's lap with his head buried in her neck the whole time. I couldn't take my eyes off him. I just felt so sad for him. It just didn't seem like him. I kept wanting him to jump up and run over and goose the preacher or something.

The next day at the homecoming service, he was still really quiet but seemed to be doing better. He wasn't crying or clinging to his mother any more. Nobody would have blamed the Harpers if they hadn't come to worship at all, but Little Zeph's daddy really wanted to be there. In fact, he took his father's place in giving the anniversary sermon. And, believe it or not, I listened close to what he had to say.

In fact, the whole sanctuary was completely silent as he stepped up to the pulpit. "Brothers and sisters," he said, "I don't want you to think I'm sad today. My father was a good man and he lived a good life. A good, *long* life. Oh, and how he loved this church throughout his life! He loved it so much that I suspect we don't even need him here to tell us the stories of our past. He has told them to us so often that we all know them by heart. In fact, I suspect if he were here and stepped up to this sacred pulpit and saw all of your faces, he might have decided not to say a word of what he had planned about the past. He would have looked out over a gathering of Methodist and Baptist, blacks and whites, brothers and sisters all, and would have said something like, "God has taken our judgment away. The Lord *is* in your midst here and now. There is too much to celebrate in the present to focus on the past. The Lord your God is in our midst!"

And people looked around at each and smiled a little. It was a quiet sort of happiness for a few minutes as everyone just took in the divine presence that filled the moment.

It was quiet, that is, until Little Zeph jumped up. I couldn't believe he was still going to go through with his plan. He ran up to the front of the sanctuary, and everyone held their breath because they knew Little Zeph's behavior patterns as well as they knew his grandfather's well-worn stories. And then Little Zeph did it. He shouted out, "Baptize me!" There was sort of a communal "Huh?" in response, and he said, "Daddy is right. If Gramps were here today, I don't think he would talk about the past. But he wouldn't have just talked about the present either. Gramps would have said that God has been with us on our long journey, through thick and thin, and God will be with us on the journey ahead! My Gramps was baptized on the day this church got started. I want to be baptized on the day we start over!"

And people in the congregation started saying, "Amen" and "Hallelujah" and "Thank you, Lord, for bringing us home."

So the pastor walked over to the baptismal font with Little Zeph and invited his family to come up and stand with him. And then he invited the other pastors to join him. And when the Methodist pastor said, "I baptize you in the name of the Father and of the Son and of the Holy Spirit," the Baptist pastor and the black pastor laid hands on Little Zeph, too.

And when the preacher said, "Amen," the choir—made up of members from all three churches—burst into

> *Joy to the world, the Lord is come!*
> *Let earth receive her King;*
> *let every heart prepare him room*
> *and heaven and nature sing.*

And I'm not sure anybody else saw, but I noticed that, right as we sang "let every heart prepare . . ." a single, little baby frog jumped out of Little Zeph's shirt pocket and splashed into the baptismal font.

MONDAY–TUESDAY, DECEMBER 15–16
Finish Developing Sermon for Advent 4

I received positive response to yesterday's sermon, but then again I always get positive responses to story-sermons . . . which always make me suspicious of them. Do they "preach" or are they just "entertaining"? But a couple of the comments did specifically relate the story to our current conversation.

Because of the holiday season, however, Second Church had scheduled no other formal conversations about the direction the church needed to head until after the New Year. Still, over the holidays, different groups in the congregation were having Christmas parties, at which informal conversations *about* our formal conversation often arose. The comments usually added little new content but offered me a sense of how important the congregation was coming to think this conversation was. Most seemed pleased with the progress but also unsure of, and a little concerned about, where it was leading us.

This congregational turn to Christmas parties and all of the talking about the conversation even though the formal conversation had paused was on my mind as I returned to the work on my sermon on Luke 1:39–56 for Advent 4 on Monday morning. Also, as I looked over my brainstorming notes from the previous Thursday, I began considering the possibility of using this sermon to tie together some threads that ran through the other three sermons in Advent in order to undergird the unity of the sermons and to prepare the congregation to shift from Advent to Christmas:

> In the Advent 1 sermon, I spoke of the New Year. It might be helpful to allude back to this and the passing of time (4 weeks).
>
> In all three sermons, I have referred to music (Advent 1: "Auld Lang Syne"; Advent 2: "Amazing Grace"; Advent 3: "Joy to the World"). I could perhaps show how Christmas carols miss the social implications of the birth story, or how we miss the social implications of some Christmas carols (e.g., "It Came Upon the Midnight Clear," "Once in Royal David's City," "Down to Earth," "Mary Had a Baby," "Sing a Different Song," "Good King Wenceslas").
>
> How do I continue to interpret eschatology for the congregation? I have referred to the End (with a capital E) a couple of times— should I repeat that phrase? In the Advent 1 sermon I spoke of beginning at the End; I could talk now of ending Advent to prepare for the beginning (birth).
>
> The theme of the future direction of Second Church's ministry has been an element in or behind each sermon thus far.
>
> There is a theme of hospitality running through all three Advent sermons thus far. How does hospitality fit in with the themes of the Magnificat? Or perhaps with Mary and Elizabeth's meeting?
>
> After having worked through Hebrews in late-Ordinary Time and having focused on a more individual, existential approach to soteriology, in the Advent sermons I have focused on the social, political, and economic aspects of Christianity's understanding of salvation.

The more I reflected on the ideas floating around in my head, the more I imagined a sermon in the basic form of (or at least the logic of) an antithesis, moving from "You always thought . . ." to "But another way to see it is. . . ." But I still didn't feel I had some controlling idea, image, or metaphor in mind to make the sermon "work." I started playing with pieces of the sermon hoping the bigger picture would come together. Although most of what I wrote would not end up in the sermon itself, it helped get a basic movement of the sermon in mind:

We usually think of the birth of Jesus as a sweet, sentimental scene. . . .

But Mary, a pregnant, unmarried woman, near the bottom of the social ladder, thinks of the birth of Jesus as a radical reversal of the status quo. . . .

So sure of the reversal is she that she speaks of the future in the past tense.

We tell the story of Christmas not simply to remember God's past, but to envision God's future.

I also decided to use Christmas music as a theme through the sermon, and at the Monday staff meeting I told the minister of music about my ideas. She suggested that instead of simply talking about music, why not incorporate music into the sermon? I usually avoid singing in the sermon, but together we thought of ways to use piano in the background of parts of the sermon and a vocal soloist in other parts. One of the songs I mentioned from my list was "Mary Had a Baby." This led the director of Christian education to suggest that we highlight that song, since earlier staff discussions of race had led him to explore an adult Sunday school curriculum the church might want to use in the future that relates Advent themes and African American spirituals. We agreed to highlight this spiritual.

Thanks to the conversation I had with the other staff members about my ideas on Monday, I was able to write a draft of the sermon on Tuesday morning with much more ease. Before laying aside my work, I e-mailed a copy of the draft to the minister of music to help her prepare the musical elements of the sermon.

Wednesday, December 17
Exegesis for Epiphany
I turned now to the task of exegesis for the Second Sunday after Christmas, which we had decided to celebrate as Epiphany Sunday. The lection on which I was to focus was Matt. 2:1–12. I explored the implications of the revelation of Christ's birth to Gentile astrologers and considered the political nature of the broader literary context of the scene in which King Herod and King Jesus are set in contrast.

Thursday, December 18
Review for Advent 4

Develop Focus & Imagery for Christmas 1
I had set aside extra sermon preparation time in my appointment calendar on this day, because the minister of music, the soloist, and I met to

walk through Sunday's sermon. We rehearsed the sermon in detail to coordinate our parts.

After rehearsal, I turned to the task of determining a focus for the sermon on John 1:1–18 for the First Sunday after Christmas. After the kinds of sermons that I have preached through Advent, and the musical and sacramental celebration we would have on Christmas Eve, I decided it would be appropriate for the First Sunday of Christmas (and the smaller congregation that will be present) to offer a teaching sermon about the doctrine of the incarnation. I brainstormed about how to focus such a sermon, how to use John's prologue but not limit the sermon to the scope of the passage, and what imagery and language might be helpful in unpacking this doctrine and demonstrating its significance for a Christian understanding of contemporary life.

FRIDAY–SATURDAY, DECEMBER 19–20
Days Off

SUNDAY, DECEMBER 21
Preach on Advent 4
I preach the following sermon on Luke 1:39–56:

Well, the first candle we lit is almost gone, the fourth candle is now burning bright, and only the Christ candle in the middle of the wreath remains to be lit. For three weeks, we have resisted well the secularization of Christmas in which the holiday season is initiated by the appearance of Santa Claus at the end of the Thanksgiving Day parade. Our homes and cars may be filled with Christmas carols, but in worship we have sung Advent hymns. But now with Christmas just around the corner, our Advent thoughts turn more and more from the coming of God in general to the coming of God in the birth of Christ. And in worship "O Come, O Come, Emmanuel" fades away while "O Come, All Ye Faithful" is being cued up. [PIANO BEGINS TO PLAY A MEDLEY OF CHRISTMAS MUSIC BEGINNING WITH "O COME, ALL YE FAITHFUL."]

Yes, the sounds of Christmas have arrived in worship as the beginning of the twelve days of Christmas draws near. And what a wonderful picture of Christ's birth those familiar melodies paint. It must have been a beautiful, quiet night. Not a cloud in the sky, not a mouse was stirring. Up until this point Mary has experienced no morning sickness, no bloating, no cramps. The ride to Bethlehem on a donkey when she is full term is no more difficult than soaking in a warm tub. And the delivery certainly isn't worthy of the label "labor." No grunting. No sweating. No difficulty breathing. No struggles not to push and then to push. No yelling at Joseph . . . or at God. None of that would be fitting for the Holy Mother. Ten minutes tops, and Jesus is in the world. It's a divine birth.

And Jesus, well, as one carol makes clear, no crying he makes. This night is the most peaceful, serene night in history. Jesus is perfect and arrives without blemish, without mess, certainly without having to be smacked on the bottom. All that is needed is to wrap the little, low-maintenance darling in swaddling cloths. You don't even need diapers, for surely the savior of the world, the one who is fully divine and fully human, is born potty trained! [PIANO FADES. ENDS IN DISCHORDANT FASHION.]

But months before Jesus is born, indeed just under nine months before Jesus is born, Mary sings a different tune. [PIANO BEGINS TO PLAY "MARY, DID YOU KNOW?" WHICH WAS SUNG EARLIER IN THE SERVICE.] Mary has come to visit her kinswoman Elizabeth, who is also pregnant, actually more pregnant than she is. When she is greeted by Elizabeth (and by John for that matter) with a celebration of the fact that she is pregnant with the Lord, Mary joins the long line of prophets that include Jeremiah and Malachi and Zephaniah in speaking lyrically about what God is going to do. But her lyrics don't speak of God's entry into the world as if it were going to be accompanied by a peaceful, easy feeling. Jesus may be the one destined to establish peace on earth, but the process leading to peace will be anything but peaceful, because there is no such thing as peace without justice. And it is rare that justice comes into the world without screaming and gasping for air.

Mary sings a prophetic song that says, Through the coming of Christ, God will turn everything upside down. So confident is she that the status quo will be overturned that she speaks of what God is going to do through Jesus in language of God's having already done it! She sings about the future using the past tense:

> God's mercy is for those who fear God
>   from generation to generation.
> God has shown strength with God's arm;
>   God has scattered the proud in the thoughts of their hearts.
> God has brought down the powerful from their thrones,
>   and lifted up the lowly;
> God has filled the hungry with good things,
>   and sent the rich away empty.

(Luke 1:50–53)

Mary knows better than to expect the arrival of salvation to be a smooth landing. After all, she is a Jewish woman in the ancient Roman Empire. She is marginalized in numerous ways. As a Jew she is part of a conquered people living under the military occupation of a stronger, mightier nation. The *Pax Romana* means peace for Rome by suppressing and oppressing any who would challenge their superiority. Moreover, as a woman, Mary was near the bottom of the social ladder, standing above only slaves and young children. Women were considered property of either their fathers or their husbands. But Mary is not just a woman; she is an unmarried woman who is pregnant. Surely she knows that for salvation to come to her, it must be more than a promise of pearly gates and golden streets in some ethereal by and by. Salvation requires that her marginalizing situation be addressed! The lowly must be lifted up! The hungry must be filled with good things! Real life inequity must receive a divine response if she is going to call it salvation! And she prophetically interprets the child whom she will bring into the world as the one who will bring *that kind* of salvation into the world.

And indeed, when Mary does give birth to Jesus, there are all kinds of signs that God has come in Christ to reclaim those discarded by society. [PIANO TRANSISTION INTO "ANGELS WE HAVE HEARD ON HIGH."] Jesus is born to a family displaced by the Roman Empire. He is born in the unclean environment of a stable. Forget about all of those Precious-Moments nativity scenes you see all the time and imagine a barn full of animals belonging to the guests who have filled the inn. Imagine the smell of cow manure, the texture of the hay on the ground that has been trampled underfoot and underhoof so much that even the goats won't eat it now, and the sight of flies swarming around the feeding trough that is rarely rinsed out.

And when the angels sing, "Glory to God in the highest and peace on earth," they don't appear on stage at the Kennedy Center in a command performance before the ruler of Judea. They go out into the fields, where the minimum wage hirelings who get stuck with the night shift are watching someone else's sheep. The savior, Christ the Lord, has come as a sign *for them*. They shall be lifted up. Their bellies shall be filled. They will receive mercy. [PIANO FADES.]

"Those who do not learn from the past are destined to repeat it." We need to get rid of the bad habit of thinking of Christmas as something that happened and instead think about it as something that is going to happen. Something we pray will happen. Something we open ourselves to allowing God to use us to make happen.

As Mary used the past tense to describe what God is going to do in the future, so we need retell the old, old story of Jesus' birth over and over again, not to remember what God once did but to claim a vision of what God promises to do.

And the sweet tunes and gentle lyrics we usually associate with Christmas don't do that very well. Oh, I don't want to get rid of those songs— I love those songs. And they do offer some significant interpretations of what it means for us to claim that God is with us in the birth of Christ. But they also omit significant implications of what it means to claim that God enters the world in the birth of Jesus in a radically different way than God has ever been present with the world before. So we need to supplement our favorite carols with other Christmas songs that sound like Mary's song of reversal. [PIANO BEGINS PLAYING "MARY HAD A BABY."] Songs that envision a Christmas future in which those living in gated communities and those living in federal housing projects trade places; a Christmas future where those who are constantly throwing away food that has spoiled in their fridge trade places with those who get their daily bread from dumpsters; a Christmas future where those above the glass ceiling will be brought down and those below the poverty line will be lifted up; God's future where those who hoard piles of money that say "In God we trust" will be scattered and those who pray that God help them make it from paycheck to paycheck will receive mercy. We need some new Christmas songs in our repertoire if we are going to be faithful to the full breadth of the Christmas vision of salvation. Songs like this one: [SOLOIST SINGS "MARY HAD A BABY."]

Mary had a baby. Oh my Lord!
Mary had a baby. Oh my Lord!
Oh, Mary had a baby. Oh my Lord!
The people keep a-comin' and the train done gone.

What did she name him? Oh my Lord!
What did she name him? Oh my Lord!
What did she name him? Oh my Lord!
The people keep a-comin' and the train done gone.

She named him Jesus. Oh my Lord!
She named him Jesus. Oh my Lord!
She named him Jesus. Oh my Lord!
The people keep a-comin' and the train done gone.

This spiritual was a work song sung by the slaves to keep the rhythm of manual labor moving along. It was also basic Christian education. Like many spirituals, it teaches basic elements of the Christian faith to a people who were denied the opportunity to learn to read the Bible for themselves. "Mary Had a Baby" tells the story of Christmas in question-and-answer fashion:

> Mary had a baby
> What did she name him?
> She named him Jesus.
> Where was he born?
> He was born in a stable.

In this way the song doesn't sound that different from any other Christmas carol we sing. But then there's that odd refrain at the end of each verse: "The people keep a-comin' and the train done gone." What in the world does a train have to do with the birth of Jesus? If this puzzles you, don't be surprised. The slave owner and field managers didn't catch it either. "Stupid slaves," they must have thought. "There were no trains back in Jesus' time."

But the slaves who sang this song were doing exactly what Renaissance artists did when they painted the nativity scene with everyone dressed in medieval clothes and when the stable scenery resembled the hills around Naples—they were interpreting the story in a way that reflected their historical reality. There are train references scattered throughout slave songs, and the references speak of the hope that the underground railroad held for freedom from slavery: liberation from racial and economic and physical oppression. "Mary had a baby, oh my Lord! The people keep a-comin' and the train done gone." People who carry the weight of the world know that the Christmas story is more than simply about Jesus' birth way back when. It is supposed to be about *our* rebirth.

And like Mary, the slaves who sing this song are so certain that God's salvation is just around the corner that they use the past tense to speak of God's future. While working someone else's fields, growing someone else's food, having someone else's babies, cleaning someone else's home, being someone else's property, they do not sing, "Mary had a baby and the train is going to come some day." They sing, "Mary had a baby and the train *done gone*!" We retell the ancient story of Christmas each year not simply to remember God's past, but to celebrate God's future.

God has shown strength with God's arm;
  God has scattered the proud in the thoughts of their hearts.
God has brought down the powerful from their thrones,
  and lifted up the lowly;
God has filled the hungry with good things,
  and sent the rich away empty.

(Luke 1:51–53)

[SOLOIST, PREACHER, AND CONGREGATION SING "MARY HAD A BABY."]

Notes

Acknowledgments

1. This lecture was published as "Pulpit in the Round: The Authority of the Pastor-Preacher in a Conversational Homiletic," *Lexington Theological Quarterly* 39, no. 1 (2004): 47–59.

Foreword

1. E.g., M. Lattke, "*homilía*," *Exegetical Dictionary of the New Testament*, ed. Horst Balz and Gerhard Schneider, tr. James W. Thompson and John W. Medendorp, 2:509–10 (Grand Rapids: Wm. B. Eerdmans Publishing Co., 1981).

Chapter 1: Sermons and Conversation

1. Theodore Zeldin, *Conversation: How Talk Can Change Our Lives* (Mahwah, N.J.: HiddenSpring, 1998), 56.
2. In *Postmodernism, Reason and Religion* (London: Routledge, 1992), 22, Ernest Gellner says, "Postmodernism is a contemporary movement. It is strong and fashionable. Over and above this, it is not altogether clear what the devil it is"; quoted in Alyce M. McKenzie, "Different Strokes for Different Folks: America's Quintessential Postmodern Proverb," in *The Academy of Homiletics: Papers of the Annual Meeting* (Durham, N.C.: Academy of Homiletics, 1994), 159.
3. Ronald J. Allen, Barbara Shires Blaisdell, and Scott Black Johnston, *Theology for Preaching: Authority, Truth and Knowledge of God in a Postmodern Ethos* (Nashville: Abingdon Press, 1997).
4. Paul Lakeland, *Postmodernity: Christian Identity in a Fragmented Age*, Guides to Theological Inquiry (Minneapolis: Fortress Press, 1997).
5. Walter Brueggemann characterizes this intellectual situation in three overarching ways: "Our knowing is inherently contextual"; "Contexts are quite local, and the more one generalizes, the more one loses or fails to notice context"; "Knowledge is inherently pluralistic, a cacophony of claims, each of which rings true to its own advocates"; *Texts Under Negotiation: The Bible and Postmodern Imagination* (Minneapolis: Fortress Press, 1993), 6–12.

6. Sharon Parks, *The Critical Years: The Young Adult Search for a Faith to Live By* (San Francisco: Harper & Row, 1986).

7. There are, of course, analogous approaches being proposed in relation to postmodernism; e.g., Craig A. Loscalzo, *Apologetic Preaching: Proclaiming Christ to a Postmodern World* (Downers Grove, Ill.: InterVarsity Press, 2000).

8. Although overstated, Alan Kelcher's stronger claim that a new paradigm of conversational preaching is developing as a postmodern response to the New Homiletic is well taken; see "Conversational Preaching: The First Postmodern Homiletics?" in *The Academy of Homiletics: Papers of the Annual Meeting* (St. Louis, Mo.: Academy of Homiletics, 2001), 393–401.

9. Examples of such comments are collected in Craig A. Loscalzo's essay on sermon feedback found in *Best Advice for Preaching*, ed. John S. McClure (Minneapolis: Fortress Press, 1998), 138–39.

10. These categories are neither exhaustive nor exact. Some of the authors could be placed in more than one category. Nevertheless, the taxonomy is useful for demonstrating the range of options available in the literature. For brief discussions of a range of methods for getting the congregation involved in the sermon, see Scott W. Alexander, *The Relational Pulpit: Closing the Gap between Preacher and Pew* (Boston: Skinner House Books, 1993), 95–107.

11. E.g., William D. Thompson and Gordon C. Bennett, *Dialogue Preaching* (Valley Forge, Pa.: Judson Press, 1969) and J. Daniel Baumann, "Dialogue Preaching," in *An Introduction to Contemporary Preaching* (Grand Rapids: Baker Book House, 1972), 257–73.

12. Bernard J. Lee, "Shared Homily: Conversation That Puts Communities at Risk," in *Alternative Futures for Worship: The Eucharist*, ed. Bernard J. Lee (Collegeville, Minn.: Liturgical Press, 1987), 157–174. For a more recent but less critical argument for dialogue sermons, see Tim Stratford, *Interactive Preaching: Opening the Word Then Listening*, Grove Worship Series (Cambridge: Grove Press, 1998).

13. Indeed Philip J. McBrien applies Lee's approach to Christian education in "Conversation: A Discipline for Studying and Teaching the Sunday Lectionary," *Religious Education* 85, no. 3 (1990): 424–35.

14. Dietrich Ritschl, *A Theology of Preaching* (Richmond: John Knox Press, 1960), 117–34, 149–57.

15. Browne Barr, *Parish Back Talk* (Nashville: Abingdon Press, 1964), see esp. 74–82.

16. Merrill R. Abbey briefly discusses and develops his own suggestions for Barr's sermon seminar in *Communication in the Pulpit and Parish* (Philadelphia: Westminster Press, 1973), 89–91; and although we do not review conversation after the sermon, we can note that Abbey also offers a short discussion of sermon "talkback sessions" and "feedback teams" (91–93).

17. See, e.g., Don M. Wardlaw, "Preaching as the Interface of Two Social Worlds: The Congregation as Corporate Agent in the Act of Preaching," in *Preaching as a Social Act: Theology and Practice*, ed. Arthur Van Seters (Nashville: Abingdon Press, 1988), 55–93.

18. John S. McClure, *The Roundtable Pulpit: Where Leadership and Preaching Meet* (Nashville: Abingdon Press, 1995). See also John S. McClure, *Other-wise Preaching: A Postmodern Ethic for Homiletics* (St. Louis, Mo.: Chalice Press, 2001), 59–62, 101–113.

19. McClure even discusses bringing people outside the congregation into the conversation in "Collaborative Preaching from the Margins," *Journal for Preachers* 19, no. 4 (1996): 37–42.

20. Fred B. Craddock, *As One without Authority* (Nashville: Abingdon Press, 1971).

21. Ruel Howe, *Partners in Preaching: Clergy and Laity in Dialogue* (New York: Seabury Press, 1967); this homiletical work is built on Howe's earlier pastoral work, *The Miracle of Dialogue* (New York: Seabury Press, 1963).

22. George Swank, *Dialogical Style in Preaching* (Valley Forge, Pa.: Judson Press, 1981).

23. Lucy Atkinson Rose, *Sharing the Word: Preaching in the Roundtable Church* (Louisville, Ky.: Westminster John Knox Press, 1997).

24. John A. Broadus, *On the Preparation and Delivery of Sermons*, rev. by Jesse Burton Weatherspoon (New York: Harper & Brothers, 1944). Revised again by Vernon L. Stanfield (San Francisco: Harper, 1979).

25. C. H. Dodd, *The Apostolic Preaching and Its Developments: Three Lectures* (Chicago: Willett, Clark & Co., 1937).

26. See Karl Barth, *The Preaching of the Gospel*, trans. B. E. Hooke (Philadelphia: Westminster Press, 1963); and idem, *Homiletics*, trans. Geoffrey W. Bromiley and Donald E. Daniels (Louisville, Ky.: Westminster/John Knox Press, 1991).

27. Ronald J. Allen, *Interpreting the Gospel: An Introduction to Preaching* (St. Louis, Mo.: Chalice Press, 1998), 65–95.

28. Ronald J. Allen, "Preaching as Mutual Critical Correlation through Conversation," in *Purpose of Preaching*, ed. Jana Childers (St. Louis, Mo.: Chalice Press, 2004), 1–22.

29. David J. Schlafer offers a similar understanding of the sermon as sacred conversation in *Your Way with God's Word: Discovering Your Distinctive Preaching Voice* (Cambridge, Ma: Cowley Publications, 1995), 9–18.

30. A similar conversational hermeneutic using mutual critical correlation in preaching is taken by Nancy Lammers Gross in "A Paradigm Shift: From System Builder to Conversational Pastor," in *If You Cannot Preach Like Paul* (Grand Rapids: Wm. B. Eerdmans Publishing Co., 2002), 44–70.

31. See Clark M. Williamson and Ronald J. Allen, *The Teaching Minister* (Louisville, Ky.: Westminster/John Knox Press, 1991), 71–129.

32. Rose does note that in her homiletical theory there is a shift "from a focus on the effect of the individual sermon to an interest in the cumulative effects of preaching" (*Sharing the Word*, 112), but in truth she does not develop the theme in much detail.

Chapter 2: A Conversational Ecclesiology

1. L. Susan Bond, *Contemporary African American Preaching: Diversity in Theory and Style* (St. Louis, Mo.: Chalice Press, 2003), 16.

2. My use of the term "circle" is intentional. In the words of David Bohm (*On Dialogue* [London: Routledge & Kegan Paul, 1997], 15), "A basic notion for a dialogue would be for people to sit in a circle. Such a geometric arrangement doesn't favor anybody; it allows for direct communication"; see also Letty M. Russell, *Church in the Round: Feminist Interpretation of the Church* (Louisville, Ky.: Westminster/John Knox Press, 1993).

3. In "Will the Real Congregation Please Stand Up" (*Homiletic* 16, no. 2 [Winter 1991]: 3–4), Richard Thulin cites James Hopewell's approach to the congregation as discourse. Thulin writes, "Hopewell claims that the hermeneutical task is not merely

the uncovering of biblical revelation in ways that are significant for individuals: 'It is more basically the tuning of the complex discourse of a congregation so that the gospel sounds within the message of its many voices.' (Hopewell, 1987, p. 11)." See James F. Hopewell, *Congregation Stories and Structures*, ed. Barbara Wheeler (Philadelphia: Fortress Press, 1987).

4. Rebecca S. Chopp, *The Power to Speak: Feminism, Language, God* (New York: Crossroad, 1989), 85 (emphasis added).

5. Compare Richard Kean's discussion of dialogue communities in "Education through Dialogue: A Revolutionary Imperative," in *Dialogue on Education*, ed. Richard Kean (Indianapolis: Bobbs-Merrill, 1967), 64–81.

6. John B. Cobb, *Reclaiming the Church: Where the Mainline Church Went Wrong and What to Do about It* (Louisville, Ky.: Westminster John Knox Press, 1997), 22–31.

7. Ibid., 31; cf. Loren Mead, *The Once and Future Church* (Washington, D.C.: Alban Institute, 1991): "In the age of Christendom, the work of theology became more and more an enterprise of the academy and its professionals and less and less relevant to everyday life. The theological frontier was addressed in learned study and in the library, but the ordinary Christian had little knowledge of its usefulness. . . . In the new *ecclesia* the primary theologians have to be the laity because they are on the missionary frontier" (56).

8. See Mark K. Smith's discussion of this matter under the heading "Dialogue and Conversation," at http://www.infed.org/biblio/b-dialog.htm, accessed March 19, 2004.

9. Taken from a list of contrasts between dialogue and debate published by The Study Circle Resource Center and based on a paper by Shelley Berman (http://www.co-intelligence.org/P-dialogue.html, accessed March 19, 2004).

10. Compare Michael A. Cowan and Bernard J. Lee, *Conversation, Risk and Conversion: The Inner and Public Life of Small Christian Communities* (Maryknoll, N.Y.: Orbis Books, 1997), where they write, "It is no etmylogical fluke that conversation and conversion have the same Latin roots from which we have pressed both words into English. Throughout our lives our conversations change us, move us, and often convert us. . . . Conversion always involves interaction with another or with others. It is not a simple, individual 'turn around.' It is a turn we take in the company of others" (2–3).

11. The Co-Intelligence Institute distinguishes between transactional conversations in which we know exactly what we are talking about and where we are headed and transformational conversations in which "something has shifted by the end of it—whether we are aware of it or not—and that shift could not have happened without these 'four unknowns' being present—not knowing what topics we would address and what solutions we'd come up with, and not knowing what we and our world would be like at the end." See http://www.co-intelligence.org/P-dialogue.html, accessed March 19, 2004.

12. In "Dialogue—A Proposal," David Bohm, Donald Factor, and Peter Garrett argue that dialogue "is not concerned with deliberately trying to alter or change behavior nor to get the participants to move toward a predetermined goal. Any such attempt would distort and obscure the processes that the Dialogue has set out to explore. Nevertheless, changes do occur because observed thought behaves differently from unobserved thought" (http://www.infed.org/archives/e-texts/bohm_dialogue.htm, accessed March 19, 2004.) Cf. also Bohm, *On Dialogue*: "The communicative virtues

... include such qualities as tolerance, patience, an openness to give and receive criticism, the inclination to admit that one may be mistaken, the desire to reinterpret or translate one's own concerns in a way that makes them comprehensible to others, the self-imposition of restraint in order that others may have a turn to speak, and— often neglected as a key element in dialogue—the willingness and ability to listen thoughtfully and attentively. As a process, dialogue requires a willingness to re-examine our own presuppositions and to compare them with those of others; to become less dogmatic about the belief that the way the world appears to us is necessarily the way the world is" (42).

13. In "Talk to Me: Talk Ethics and Erotics" (in *Talk, Talk, Talk: The Cultural Life of Everyday Conversation*, ed. S. I. Salamensky [London: Routledge & Kegan Paul, 2001], 63–75), Carle Kaplan discusses the critique of positive, even utopian, images of social and political dialogue as comprising equality, reciprocity, and deep satisfaction. The transformative power of discourse is curtailed and potentially usurped by power relations between persons and groups of different 'footings' or social status.

14. Of course, if honesty is a quality of the church's conversation, at times speech may be necessarily painful. Conversions, both dramatic and minute, include not only the excitement and joy of embracing new ideas, views, relationships, and experiences, but often also the mournful and difficult task of turning away from old ideas, views, relationships, and experiences. The *goal* of the church's conversation, however, should never be to inflict harm but to move through painful revelations to healing newness (as a surgeon inflicts symptoms of pain to cure a more significant illness).

15. Hans-George Gadamer, *Truth and Method* (New York: Crossroad, 1982), 186–88, 347, 354–56, 362–88, 538–39.

16. David Tracy, *Plurality and Ambiguity: Hermeneutics, Religion, Hope* (Chicago: University of Chicago Press, 1984), 19, 23–24, 27, 30–31, 35, 74–75, 92, 106, 109, 116–17, 121–23, 127, 132–36, 138. Cf. Joseph Webb's use of Kenneth Burke's description of interpretation as conversation with a text in *Preaching and the Challenge of Pluralism* (St. Louis, Mo.: Chalice Press, 1998), 83–102.

17. See Roy Herndon Steinhoffsmith's critique of this move in "Dialogue: Hermeneutic and Practical," *Pastoral Psychology* 45, no. 6 (1997): 439–49.

18. E.g., Paulo Friere, *Pedagogy of the Oppressed*, trans. Myra Bergman Ramos (New York: Seabury Press, 1970); Nicolas Burbules, *Dialogue in Teaching: Theory and Practice* (New York: Teachers College Press, 1993); Tony Jeffs and Mark K. Smith, *Informal Education: Conversation, Democracy and Learning* (Ticknall, Derbyshire: Education Now Books, 1999), and see http://www.infed.org, accessed March 19, 2004. Cf. also R. Wardhaugh, *How Conversation Works* (Oxford: Basil Blackwell Publisher, 1985); Wolfram Bublitz, *Supportive Fellow-Speakers and Cooperative Conversations* (Philadelphia: John Benjamins, 1988); J. Vella, *Learning to Listen, Learning to Teach: The Power of Dialogue in Educating Adults* (San Francisco: Jossey-Bass, 1994); Peter Burke, *The Art of Conversation* (Ithaca, N.Y.: Cornell University Press, 1993); Ronald C. Arnett, *Dialogic Education: Conversation about Ideas and between Persons* (Carbondale, Ill.: Southern Illinois University Press, 1992). Robert Grudin, *On Dialogue: An Essay in Free Thought* (Boston: Houghton Mifflin, 1996); David Bohm, *On Dialogue*; T. Zeldin, *Conversation: How Talk Can Change Your Life* (London: Harvill, 1998); Christopher M. Clark, *Talking Shop: Authentic Conversation and Teacher Learning* (New York: Teachers College Press, 2001).

19. A recent overview essay of the discussion in educational circles can be found in Helen Colley, Phil Hodkinson, and Janice Malcolm, "Non-formal Learning: Mapping the Conceptual Terrain, A Consultation Report" (http://www.infed.org/archives/e-texts/colley_informal_learning.htm, accessed March 19, 2004).

20. Cf. Burbules, *Dialogue in Teaching*, 7: "The central question . . . is whether a theory and practice of dialogue that respond to the postmodern critique are possible. I hope to suggest an approach to dialogue that challenges hierarchies and traditional conceptions of teacher authority; that is tolerant and supportive of diversity; that does not rely on teleological presumptions of right answers and final truths; that does not rest on isolated individual efforts, but on mutual and reciprocal communicative relations; and that keeps the conversation open, both in the sense of open-endedness and in the sense of inviting a range of voices and styles of communication within it."

21. Ibid., 19–20; see also Wardhaugh, *How Conversation Works*, 2–3.

22. Cf. Wardhaugh, *How Conversation Works*, 5–7, 18.

23. As Friere (*Pedagogy of the Oppressed*, 79–80) puts it, "Founding itself upon love, humility, and faith, dialogue becomes a horizontal relationship of which mutual trust between the dialoguers is the logical consequence. . . . Whereas faith in man is an *a priori* requirement for dialogue, trust is established by dialogue."

24. Cf. Wardhaugh, *How Conversation Works*, 63–64.

25. Burbules (*Dialogue in Teaching*, 27) writes, "While many are drawn to dialogue as a pedagogical approach because of the egalitarian sentiments, equality per se is not necessary for dialogue to exist. . . . The fact that participants are unequal in knowledge, experience, or intelligence is not a detriment to the possibilities of dialogue—on the contrary, it often helps explain why partners are drawn into the relation with one another."

26. Friere, *Pedagogy of the Oppressed*, 78.

27. Martin Buber, *I and Thou*, tr. Walter Kaufman (New York: Charles Scribner's Sons, 1970); see also *Between Man and Man*, tr. R. G. Smith (London: Routledge & Kegan Paul, 1947), where Buber writes, "There is genuine dialogue—no matter whether spoken or silent—where each of the participants really has in mind the other or others in their present and particular being and turns to them with the intention of establishing a living mutual relation between himself and them. There is technical dialogue, which is prompted solely by the need of objective understanding. And there is monologue disguised as dialogue, in which two or more men, meeting in space, speak each with himself in strangely tortuous and circuitous ways and yet imagine they have escaped the torment of being thrown back on their own resources" (19).

28. Cf. Freire's critique of a "banking" concept of education: "Education thus becomes an act of depositing, in which the students are depositories and the teacher is the depositor. Instead of communicating, the teacher issues communiqués and makes deposits which the students patiently receive, memorize, and repeat" (*Pedagogy of the Oppressed*, 58).

29. Wardhaugh writes, "Conversation involves a kind of trade-off between public benefit and personal profit: you have to give in order to get" (*How Conversation Works*, 60); or per Arnett: "An emphasis on persons is a reminder that discussion of ideas is not initiated in the abstract, but with others, attempting to contribute to human life,

aesthetically, emotionally, economically, and practically" (*Dialogic Education*, 22, see also 95–97).

30. Burbules, *Dialogue in Teaching*, 7–8.

31. See John McClure's discussion of symmetrical and asymmetrical relationships in *The Roundtable Pulpit*, 42–43, 52–54.

32. Arnett quotes Paul Keller as stating that "the true test of dialogue is in disagreement, not mutual understanding" (*Dialogic Education*, 27).

33. See Wardhaugh, *How Conversation Works*, 3; or as Jeffs and Smith, *Informal Education* comment, "Conversation . . . is not about trying to win an argument. Rather, conversation is about understanding and learning. This does not mean that we avoid debate and challenge. What it does involve, though, is constantly being open to the possible truth of what others are saying. This makes it a risky business. To be open to what others are saying we have to bring our own beliefs and feelings into play. In other words, we have to enter conversations ready to change our view of things" (http://www.infed.org, accessed March 19, 2004). See also Cowan and Lee, *Conversation, Risk and Conversion*, 84–91.

34. Arnett asserts, "Dialogue requires us to bring our own perspective to a conversation, not as the *only* perspective, but with the knowledge that new insight comes when both parties bring their uniqueness to the conversation" (*Dialogic Education*, 78).

35. Cf. Friere, "The dialogical character of education as the practice of freedom does not begin when the teacher-student meets with the students-teachers in a pedagogical situation, but rather when the former first asks himself *what* he will dialogue with the latter *about*" (*Pedagogy of the Oppressed*, 81–82).

36. Mary Catherine Hilkert, *Naming Grace: Preaching and the Sacramental Imagination* (New York: Continuum, 1997), 46.

37. At this point, Hilkert (ibid., 32) is quoting Karl Rahner (*Theological Investigation* [Baltimore: Helicon, 1967], 313).

38. Paul Scherer, *For We Have This Treasure* (New York: Harper & Brothers, 1944), 112.

39. While this emphasis on Christian language has affinities with the cultural-linguistic approach of George Lindbeck as found in *The Nature of Doctrine: Religion and Theology in a Postliberal Age* (Philadelphia: Westminster Press, 1984), the direction it is taken in terms of naming divine presence in a public, postmodern conversation between all aspects of human existence and the process of Christian meaning making is quite different from postliberal approaches to preaching; contrast my proposal with the views of Stanley Hauerwas and William Willimon in *Resident Aliens: Life in the Christian Colony* (Nashville: Abingdon Press, 1989) and Charles L. Campbell in *Preaching Jesus: New Directions for Homiletics in Hans Frei's Postliberal Theology* (Grand Rapids: Wm. B. Eerdmans Publishing Co., 1997).

40. Burbules, *Dialogue in Teaching*, 80–82.

41. At another point in his work, Burbules comments on the dilemma inherent in the need for active participation: "The dialogue game requires participants or contenders who are different enough to provide sufficient tensions for the to-and-fro movement to have interest and pleasure; yet when this contention comes to be seen as a struggle or battle, the enjoyment is destroyed. To put this in less analogical terms, the development of new beliefs, new understandings, or new appreciations requires conflict (and a tolerance for conflict) between what we already 'know' and some new information or perspectives that challenge us. . . . Yet a cacophony of an excess of

conflict is directly counterproductive to this goal, making us *less* able or willing to encounter other voices seriously. This dilemma, I believe, is inherent in communication, and we will occasionally find ourselves erring in one direction (encouraging the unreconciled plurality of contending voices and perspectives) or the other (assuming a greater degree of commonality and agreement than actually exists)" (Ibid., 64).

42. Michael F. Schober, "Conversational Evidence for Rethinking Meaning," *Social Research* 65, no. 3 (1998): 511–35.

43. Bohm avoids offering rules for his dialogue process but does assert some general principles, one of the most important of which is that "we must give space for each person to talk" (*On Dialogue*, 30).

44. See Friere, *Pedagogy of the Oppressed*, 66–67.

45. Burbules, *Dialogue in Teaching*, 80–81

46. Wardhaugh, *How Conversation Works*, 33.

47. John L. Locke, *The De-Voicing of Society: Why We Don't Talk to Each Other Anymore* (New York: Simon & Schuster, 1998); the following discussion summarizes pages 118–67.

48. See Robert D. Putnam, *Bowling Alone: The Collapse and Revival of American Community* (New York: Simon & Schuster, 2000).

49. Arnett writes, "Dialogue is an invitation, not a demand, nourished not so much by the guarantee that it will happen as by patience" (*Dialogic Education*, 4).

50. Bohm argues that the proper starting point for dialogue is talking *about* dialogue itself (*On Dialogue*, 6, 18).

51. While face-to-face conversation around a circle is the best scenario for give-and-take proclamation, we should not ignore opportunities to construct conversations in print (e.g., bulletins and newsletters) and electronic media (e.g., Web sites, e-mail, and on-line chat rooms).

Chapter 3: A Conversational Homiletic

1. William A. Beardslee, et al., *Biblical Preaching on the Death of Jesus* (Nashville: Abingdon Press, 1989), 32.

2. Burbules, *Dialogue in Teaching*, 31–35.

3. Cf. Jeffrey Francis Bullock, *Preaching with a Cupped Ear: Hans-Georg Gadamer's Philosophical Hermeneutics as Postmodern Wor(l)d*, Berkeley Insights in Linguistics and Semiotics 34 (New York: Peter Lang, 1999); see also Nelle Morton ("Preaching the Word," originally published in *Sexist Religion and Women of the Church—No More Silence*, ed. Alice Hageman [New York: Association Press, 1974], 29–46, collected in *The Journey Is Home* [Boston: Beacon Press, 1985], 41), who writes, "In an introduction to Faust, I remembered the writer/editor quoting Goethe saying, 'In the beginning was not the Word. In the beginning was the Act.' I blurted aloud, 'Ah! No! In the beginning was not the Word. In the beginning was the hearing!' Suddenly the whole patriarchal interpretation of word and preaching reversed themselves for me. . . . If the style of a woman's preaching was not to deliver (to proclaim) the Word but to place her ear close to the pulse of the people, then a new kind of Pentecost would be possible. Each tongue would be loosened and each would be speaking her/his own word and that word would be herself/himself."

4. Friere, *Pedagogy of the Oppressed*, 67.

5. See Fred B. Craddock's discussion of the mid-twentieth-century understanding of preaching as the Word of God regardless of whether one accepted a Barthian or Bultmannian stance (in *As One without Authority*, rev. ed. [Nashville: Abingdon Press, 1974], 37–48); see also Mary Catherine Hilkert's discussion of Barth, Bultmann, Tillich, and the New Hermeneutic theologians in "The Dialectical Imagination: The Power of the Word," in *Naming Grace*, 19–29.

6. T. H. L. Parker, *John Calvin: A Biography* (Philadelphia: Westminster Press, 1975), 89.

7. Quoted in Patrick Ferry, "Martin Luther on Preaching: Promises and Problems of the Sermon as a Source of Reformation History and as an Instrument of the Reformation," *Concordia Theological Quarterly* 54, no. 4 (1990): 270.

8. In his December 6, 2003, address to the Academy of Homiletics, "Can Preaching Be Taught," Edward Farley commented that even though neither Catholics nor Protestants refer to preaching as such, both groups consider preaching a sacrament. Indeed, for Protestants, Farley claims, there is reason to claim that preaching is treated as the primary sacrament.

9. See Fred W. Meuser, *Luther the Preacher* (Minneapolis: Augsburg, 1983), 45–47.

10. See James F. White, *Protestant Worship: Traditions in Transition* (Louisville, Ky.: Westminster/John Knox Press, 1989), 17–18.

11. For a related, yet different, critique of the understanding of the sermon as an "event" of the Word of God, see Richard Lischer, "Preaching as the Church's Language," in *Listening to the Word: Studies in Honor of Fred B. Craddock*, ed. Gail R. O'Day and Thomas G. Long (Nashville: Abingdon Press, 1993), 121–23; for a feminist critique of the hegemony of "the Word" in relation to the pulpit, see Morton, "Preaching the Word," 54–57.

12. Hilkert, *Naming Grace*, 40.

13. Cf. David Buttrick's use of a photography analogy for describing the preacher's point of view in *Homiletic: Moves and Structures* (Philadelphia: Fortress Press, 1987), 57–62.

14. Compare Fred B. Craddock's discussion of the historical, pastoral, liturgical, and theological context in *Preaching* (Nashville: Abingdon Press, 1985), 31–50; and Ronald J. Allen's discussion of the contexts of the church, the larger world, and the life of the preacher in *Interpreting the Gospel: An Introduction to Preaching* (St. Louis, Mo.: Chalice Press, 1998), 19–61.

15. For more on analyzing the congregation for the sake of preaching see Leonora Tubbs Tisdale, *Preaching as Local Theology and Folk Art* (Minneapolis: Fortress Press, 1997).

16. For help relating preaching and theology see Ronald J. Allen, *Preaching Is Believing: The Sermon as Theological Reflection* (Louisville, Ky.: Westminster John Knox Press, 2002) and Burton Z Cooper and John S. McClure, *Claiming Theology in the Pulpit* (Louisville, Ky.: Westminster John Knox Press, 2003).

17. While this statement does represent the Reformers' primary understanding of biblical preaching, it should be noted that John Calvin did use the metaphor of spectacles to describe the Bible as that through which we look to sharpen our knowledge of God, found in *Institutes of the Christian Religion*, 1.6.1, 1.14.1; ed. John T. McNeill, trans. Ford Lewis Battles, The Library of Christian Classics (Philadelphia: Westminster Press, 1960), 1:70, 1:160; for contemporary application of Calvin's metaphor see William H. Willimon, *Pastor: The Theology and Practice of Ordained Ministry* (Nashville: Abingdon, 2002), 101, 127–28; and Stephen Farris, "With the Aid of

Spectacles: Teaching Exegesis in Preaching Class," in *The Academy of Homiletics: Papers of the Annual Meeting* (Memphis, Tn.: Academy of Homiletics, 2004), 7–10.

18. To be more precise we might represent the Bible in the entirety of its composite nature as a set of lenses. Any particular biblical text chosen for a sermon would be the particular biblical lens used by the preacher on that day. Taking a snapshot of a given instance of God's presence in the world using a different biblical lens would naturally render a different (yet related) snapshot.

19. Indeed, Luther's own high theology of preaching and optimism concerning the pulpit led him to feel great disappointment about his effectiveness as a preacher; see Ferry, "Martin Luther," 265–80.

20. See n. 39 in chapter 2.

21. Kenneth Burke, "Definition of Man," in *Language as Symbolic Action* (Berkeley: University of California Press, 1966), 5.

22. Martin Heidegger, "The Nature of Language," in *On the Way to Language*, trans. Peter D. Hertz (New York: San Francisco: Harper Collins, 1971), 57–108.

23. Thomas G. Long, "Preaching about Evangelism—Faith Finding Its Voice," in *Preaching In and Out of Season*, ed. Thomas G. Long and Neely Dixon McCarter (Louisville, Ky.: Westminster/John Knox Press, 1990), 86–87; see also Long's discussion of equipping practical saints with theological vocabulary in "Preaching in the Middle of a Saintly Conversation," *Journal for Preachers* 18, no. 2 (1995): 15–21.

24. Cf. Kenneth Burke's discussion of language as terministic screens in *Language as Symbolic Action*, 44–62.

25. Contra David Buttrick's description of the "mnemonic gospel message," in *Homiletic*, 247.

26. Note the criteria concerning use of Christian language in the previous chapter.

Chapter 4: Practical Implications of a Conversational Homiletic

1. Stuart Briscoe, "Planning Preaching," in *Leadership Handbook of Preaching and Worship: Practical Insights from a Cross Section of Ministry Leaders* (Grand Rapids: Baker Book House, 1992), 52.

2. One exception is Adam Hamilton's recent description of his process of developing a plan for preaching a sermon series over time in *Unleashing the Word: Preaching with Relevance, Purpose, and Passion* (Nashville: Abingdon Press, 2003).

3. In contrast to most homiletical textbooks, Ronald J. Allen's *Interpreting the Gospel* introduces a wide range of sermon forms for students to digest at the introductory level. This text along with its companion collection of sermons, *Patterns of Preaching*, edited by Allen, gives good examples of the smorgasbord of forms he presents in the textbook.

4. E.g., see Carol Gilligan's influential study, *In a Different Voice: Psychological Theory and Women's Development* (Cambridge, Mass.: Harvard University Press, 1982).

5. E.g., Christine M. Smith, *Weaving the Sermon: Preaching in Feminist Perspective* (Louisville Ky.: Westminster/John Knox Press, 1989); Lee McGee, *Wrestling with the Patriarchs: Retrieving Women's Voices in Preaching* (Nashville: Abingdon Press, 1996); and especially Mary Donovan Turner and Mary Lin Hudson, *Saved from Silence: Finding Women's Voice in Preaching* (St. Louis, Mo.: Chalice Press, 1999).

6. E.g., David Schlafer, *Your Way with God's Word: Discovering Your Distinctive Preaching Voice* (Cambridge, Mass.: Cowley Publications, 1995).

7. Arthur N. Strahler presents such a reasoning circle (which he calls the induction/deduction feedback cycle) as the basis of the scientific method in *Understanding Science: An Introduction to Concepts and Issues* (Buffalo, N.Y.: Prometheus Books, 1992), 25–27.

8. David Buttrick, *Homiletic: Moves and Structures* (Philadelphia: Fortress Press, 1987), 133–35.

9. See O. Wesley Allen, Jr., *Good News for Tinyville: Stories of Hope and Heart* (St. Louis, Mo.: Chalice Press, 1999).

10. For an example of a long-range plan with a different theological orientation than the one offered here, see Hamilton, *Unleashing the Word*, especially 19–28.

11. For an example of a typical and helpful *weekly* schedule of sermon preparation, see Paul Scott Wilson, *The Practice of Preaching* (Nashville: Abingdon Press, 1995), 125–196.

12. The time lines used in this example process assume that to avoid pastoral burnout, preachers should hold to a basic five-day workweek that includes Sunday and four weekdays. Therefore, the counting of days includes Fridays and Saturdays as days that are not standard workdays.

13. Advent and Christmas are grouped together not only because of their obvious connection but also because of the short length of the liturgical seasons. The choosing of texts could be separated into the four Sundays of Advent and then later Christmas through Epiphany (January 6) to distinguish the seasons in the preacher's planning process. Note that for the sake of simplicity in presenting this model, the schedule does not include non-Sunday services such as Christmas Eve, Christmas Day, or Epiphany. These extra preaching occasions would require extra preparation time. However, the biblical texts should be chosen as part of the group chosen for the appropriate season.

14. Of course, the preacher may be dealing with these texts with others outside the individual sermon preparation process as various aspects of the worship service are planned. Indeed, choosing texts as part of a conversational circle instead of the preacher's choosing them alone is highly recommended if one truly wishes to develop a conversational approach to worship as a whole.

Chapter 5: A Case Study of Conversational Homiletic

1. Robin R. Meyers, *With Ears to Hear: Preaching as Self-persuasion* (Cleveland: Pilgrim Press, 1993), 29.

2. Although the schedule includes choosing texts for Christmas at this time, I treat only Advent texts in order to keep our discussion focused.

3. Taken from *A Prairie Home Companion Pretty Good Joke Book*, rev. ed. (Minneapolis: Highbridge, 2001), 143.